M

AWESOME INFECTIONS

New and

Carl Tant

D0840811

Biotech Publishing
A Division of
Plant Something Different, Inc.
Angleton, TX, USA

AWESOME INFECTIONS
New and Emerging Diseases
By Carl Tant

Published by Biotech Publishing
P. O. Box 1032
Angleton, TX 77516-1032
(281) 369-2044

Copyright © 1998 by Biotech Publishing

Printing   10 9 8 7 6 5 4 3 2 1

Library of Congress Catalog Number: 97-78295
Softcover   ISBN 1-880319-19-5

Publisher's Cataloging in Publication Data
Tant, Carl.
Awesome infections: New and emerging diseases/Carl Tant. - 1st ed.
p.cm.
Includes bibliographical references and index.
1. Diseases. 2. Viruses. I. Title.
II. Title: New and emerging diseases.
                          1998   616
RA 648.5

Cover, layout and illustration
by Tammy Kay Crask

Table of Contents

I. The Present Problem
 * The Diseases 3
 * The Spread 7
 * Natural Microbial Processes 9
 * People Factors 14
 * Ecological Changes 16
 * Pollution Problems 19
 * A New Means of Spread 19
 * A New Way to get Infected 21
 * Physician Errors 22
 * New Vectors 24
 * Combined Problems 26
 * Climate Factors 28
 * Changing Prevention Programs 29

II. Frightening Infections: The Outbreaks, Epidemics, and Pandemics
 * Avian Influenza H5N1 ("Bird Flu") 31
 * BSE: The Mad Cow Disease Group 33
 * Bunyaviruses: Sometimes The Answer is "No" 37
 * Chlamydial Infections 41
 * Cholera 43
 * Coccidioidomycosis 47
 * Cryptosporidiosis 50
 * Dengue and Dengue Hemorrhagic Fever 55
 * E. coli Infections 57
 * Genital Herpes 60
 * Giardiasis 63
 * The Hantaviruses 65
 * Legionnaires' Disease 68
 * Malaria 70
 * Myocarditis--Another New One? 74
 * Nosocomial Infections and Antibiotic Resistance 76
 * O'nyong-Nyong Fever 79
 * Pfiesteriosis 81
 * Prostatitis 82
 * Salmonellosis 84

* Tuberculosis   86
* Venezuelan Equine Encephalitis   90
* Vibrio Vulnificus - An "Impossible" Infection   92
* Yellow Fever   94
* New Disease of Non-Human Life   96

III. Control and Prevention
* Control and Prevention   98
* The Program for Prevention and Control   98
* Surveillance and Quick Response   100
* Communication   102
* Human Behavior   103
* The New Technologies   103

Epilogue   105
References   109
    Appendix A. Glossary   117
    Appendix B. Abbreviations   120
    Appendix C. Internet Resources   122
Index   126

Warning - Disclaimer

This book is not a medical textbook. It is a limited review of the scientific literature pertaining to new and emerging diseases. It is not intended to give medical advice about the diagnosis, treatment, or control of any disease. Readers are cautioned to consult licensed medical practitioners or appropriate publications for such information.

Dedication

To my two sons, John and Steven, with the hope they avoid the awesome infections.

Acknowledgment

The author gratefully acknowledges the help of some of the publisher's staff in making this work possible. These include Leanne Wagener who assisted with literature searching and provided editorial assistance; Colinda Roden kept things organized and provided much of the text entry.

The striking last minute report in the epilogue was generously provided by Dr. Martin Hugh-Jones of the Department of Epidemiology and Community Health in the Louisiana State University School of Veterinary Medicine. He also afforded some valuable insight into the problems of epidemiology in developing nations and their relationships to other countries.

Author Mary Lou Stahl (by her own definition, a non-scientist) reviewed an early version of the text for clarity.

A special thanks goes to my student, David Rambin, who reviewed an early draft and provided helpful suggestions.

THE AWESOME SCIENCE OF BIOLOGY SERIES

A Note From The Publisher

Welcome to the third volume of the Awesome Science Of Biology Series!

Today, the science of biology is changing at a rate undreamed of only one or two decades ago. The theoretical laboratory research of a year ago suddenly becomes practical application. The new knowledge creates new subdivisions of biological science. It has become difficult for scientists, even biologists, to keep up with the changes. The task of understanding the new knowledge is almost insurmountable for the non-scientist. Yet, there is a pressing necessity to understand.

The new processes and technologies are described in scientific research literature which, even if accessible, is unfamiliar to the non-scientist. The technical terminology utilized in reporting research results is more often than not the equivalent of being addressed in a foreign language for the average layperson. The alternative is often only to obtain information from the popular press. Unfortunately, much of the information is presented by writers who, themselves, do not have a science background to understand the full implications of the processes, or are seeking dramatic subjects to capture the reader's attention and sell more copies of the publication.

The goal of the ASB SERIES is to explore the new knowledge with a scientifically qualified author who can translate the technical jargon of the research literature into terms understandable by those not specialized in the discipline. Our only sources of information are interviews with scientists themselves and peer-reviewed scientific literature. No information is based on the sensational stories often found in the popular press. The sources of information are properly cited in the text and a reference list with full details of publication is provided for those who might have interest in and access to it.

For this volume only, we have deviated slightly from the strict peer reviewed literature policy. Some diseases are spreading so rapidly that it does not make sense to wait one to two years for traditional publication. Therefore, we have utilized scientifically sound electronic sources such as the Center for Disease Control, World Health Organization, and the moderated ProMED list. No popular media reports have been used.

Long technical terms are often a turn-off for people who would otherwise like to further their scientific knowledge. We do not oversimplify and attempt to eliminate such terms because we live in a technical world and new words are continually coined to describe new processes. We do attempt to explain these terms in a manner the average reader can understand.

The ASB SERIES does not pretend to be an exhaustive survey of all the scientific literature about a particular topic. That is the proper domain of literature reviews published in scientific research journals or even in review books. We have, however, made every effort to review the most pertinent and, what we feel to be, the most important reports on a subject. Sometimes, these may not be the most recent. If, for example, a scientist made a major discovery and reported it in 1987, that work will be cited. While confirmation is recognized as being important, later "me too" reports by other scientists may not be mentioned. Where research results or interpretations differ and there is legitimate scientific disagreement, the ASB Series attempts to explain all viewpoints.

A Note From The Author

Our first outline for this book neatly separated the discussions of specific diseases into two sections designated ""New" and "Re-emerging." As we delved deeper in the literature, it quickly became apparent that such a division would not work. Many of the infections classified as new by world health authorities are actually the result of variants or mutants of previously known species. A hard-ruled separation would result in redundancy and might be confusing. To make reference easier for the reader, we took the safe way out of the dilemma: alphabetize. This permits getting all the relationships and variants assembled together in Section II.

The next problem involved virus classification. Are viruses really living organisms or just remarkably complex chemical molecules? Since we do not consider this review a proper place to get mired in the issue, we ducked it by applying authors' treatments in citations. Obviously, this approach produces some inconsistencies, but they are the result of legitimate scientific disagreement.

It is a new world out there. Another issue that had to be addressed was that of form for citation and reference of electronic publications. There seem to be about as many ideas on this subject as there are scientists, librarians, English teachers, and editors. Hopefully, the method used here will make finding the original source easy. Recognize that the internet is by no means an archive and try an old-fashioned author search if the URL given no longer exists.

The fact that we have given only cursory attention to some diseases such as AIDS and Ebola Fever does not mean that we consider them unimportant. It does mean that in view of the uncountable volumes written about them, we have preferred to concentrate on the lesser known threats to humans.

Prologue

We thought the plagues were in the past. Little did we foresee awakening from our dream world of the 1950's. New treatments for infectious diseases were discovered regularly as scientists sifted through tons of soil seeking the microbes that would produce new antibiotics. There was even hope for eliminating the untreatable virus diseases as immunology emerged from its realm that many considered to be little more than scientific witchcraft. The new vaccine to prevent polio was the breakthrough long sought, the prototype of countless preventions. A new generation of doctors scoffed at strict aseptic technique. Only a few lonely voices echoed the accusation of Semmelweiss a century before at the Vienna Lying-In Hospital, "Gentleman, you are killing your patients." Massive aerial spraying of DDT was eliminating mosquito and other insect vectored diseases. We prepared to step into a world free of infectious disease.

But, the infectious agents of the Angel of Death did not disappear. They are returning newly strengthened and accompanied by new cohorts. We call their pestilences the new and emerging diseases.

They can kill us.

Section I

The Present Problem

The United Nations World Health Organization

New diseases are those which have appeared

for the first time during the last 20 years.

Emerging infections are those which have

existed, but are rapidly increasing in

incidence or geographic range.

The Diseases

The United Nations World Health Organization (WHO) definition of new and emerging diseases shown at the beginning of this section limits the problems to those which have appeared for the first time or reappeared after long periods of absences during the last twenty years.

Tables 1.1 and 1.2 on the following pages summarize the new and reemerging diseases defined by the WHO at the end of 1996. We have added a new Salmonellosis which has appeared in early 1997. Later in the year, we experienced the appearance of Pfiesteriosis and Avian Influenza H5N1. These diseases will be described in more detail in Section II.

The history of the human species is also a history of infectious disease. Pre-history processes of the microbes are revealed in fossil man. Wars have been won or lost and the history of our world has been frequently changed by epidemics too horrible to imagine.

Long before he understood the cause of transmissible infections, thinking man made efforts to control or prevent their outbreaks. The early Judaic dietary laws prescribed many sound food preparation and sanitation practices important at the time they were given. Other cultures instituted similar practices.

Today we face new threats as pathogenic microorganisms achieve survival at human expense. The devastating epidemics of the past may be only previews of what we face in the coming years.

Table 1.1. New Diseases

Microorganism Bacteria/Rickettsia	Disease	Year Appeared
Legionella pneumophila	Legionnaires' disease	1977
Campylobacter jejuni	Enteric pathogens distributed globally	1977
Toxic producing strains of Staphylococcus aureus	Toxic shock syndrome (tampon use)	1981
Escherichia coli 0157:H7	Hemorrhagic colitis; hemolytic uremic syndrome	1982
Borrelia burgdorferi	Lyme disease	1982
Helicobacter pylori	Peptic ulcer disease	1983
Ehrlichia chafeensis	Human Ehrlichiosis	1989
Vibrio cholerae 0139	New strain associated with epidemic cholera	1992
Bartonella henselae	Cat-scratch disease; bacillary angiomatosis	1992
Viruses		
Rotavirus	infantile diarrhea worldwide	1973
Parvovirus B19	Aplastic crisis in chronic hemolytic anemia	1975
Ebola Virus	Ebola hemorrhagic fever	1977
HTLV-II	Hairy cell leukemia	1982
Human immuno-deficiency virus (HIV)	Acquired immunodeficiency Syndrome (AIDS)	1983
Human herpesvirus-6 (HHV-6)	Roseola subitum	1988

Microorganism	Disease	Year Appeared
Hepatitis E	Enterically transmitted non-A, non-B hepatitis	1988
Hepatitis C	Parenterally transmitted non-A, non-B, liver infection	1989
Hantaanvirus	Hemorragic fever with renal syndrome (HRFS)	1977
Human T-lymphotropic	T-cell lymphoma-leukemia virus I (HTLV-1)	1980
Guanarito virus	Venezuelan hemorrhagic fever	1991
Sin nombre virus	Adult respiratory distress syndrome	1993
Sabia virus	Brazilian hemorrhagic fever	1994
HHV-8	Associated with Kaposi sarcoma in AIDS patients	1995
Parasite		
Cryptosporidium parvum	Acute and chronic diarrhea	1976
Enterocytozoon bieneusi	Persistent diarrhea	1985
Cyclospora cayatanensis	Persistent diarrhea	1986
Encephalitozzon hellem	Conjunctivitis, disseminated disease	1991
New species of Babesia	Atypical babesiosis	1991
Encephalitozoon cuniculi	Disseminated disease	1993

Table 1.2 Re-emerging Diseases

Diseases
Viral
Dengue/dengue hemorrhagic fever
Malaria
Rabies
Yellow Fever
Parasitic
Acanthamebiasis
Echinococcosis
Giardiasis
Neurocysticerosis
Schistosomiasis
Toxoplasmosis
Visceral leishmaniasis
Bacterial
Cholera
Diphtheria
E. coli 0157
Group A Streptococcus
Pertussis
Plague
Pneumococcal pneumonia
Salmonellosis
Trench fever
Tuberculosis

The Spread

Most new infections have their origin in a very limited environment, completely isolated from the rest of the world as though in a closet. Once the disease establishes itself in a human host, spread can be rapid as the door is opened (Fig. 1). Sometimes the spread of a disease is the result of a single simple factor; in other cases it may involve a complex series of reactions involving many characteristics. Some factors involve natural processes over which man has no control. Others involve human behaviors.

Table 1.3 lists some of the major factors involved in spread of new and emerging diseases. Now, lets consider some examples of how these conditions work alone or with others.

Table 1.3. Causes of Disease Emergence

1. Microorganisms undergo evolutionary changes
2. Known diseases invade new geographic areas
3. Known diseases attack new populations
4. Antimicrobial drug resistance develops
5. Ecologic changes bring new exposure to pathogens or vectors
6. Previously unrecognized infections are discovered
7. Increasing urbanization of populations
8. Breakdowns in public health practices
9. Slow governmental response to a problem

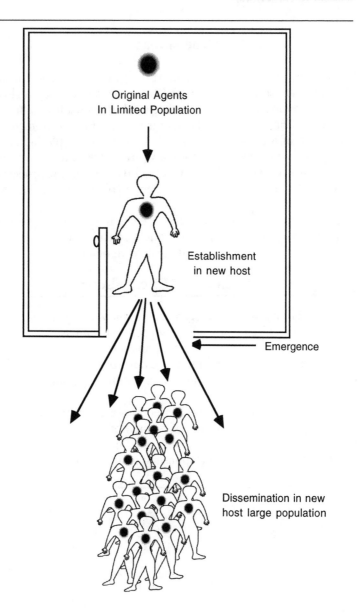

Figure 1. Emergence of Disease.

Natural Microbial Processes

Microbial evolutionary changes in the forms of adaptation and mutation are natural processes common to all forms of life. In general they cannot be changed or controlled by man. However, human factors such as the misuse of antibiotics can create conditions which encourage adaptation. Mutagenic agents released into the environment can increase the normal mutation rate.

Pandemic influenza viruses are an excellent example of natural formation of new varieties. Webster *et al* (1992) and Scholtissek *et al* (1988) have shown how a new strain of the virus originates by natural recombination of elements from related viruses present in pigs and ducks in China. The new recombinant is capable of infecting humans. Since it is new, the human host has had no previous exposure and consequently has no natural immunity. Figure 1.2 shows how such recombination occurs. These are ideal conditions for rapid spread of the new strain.

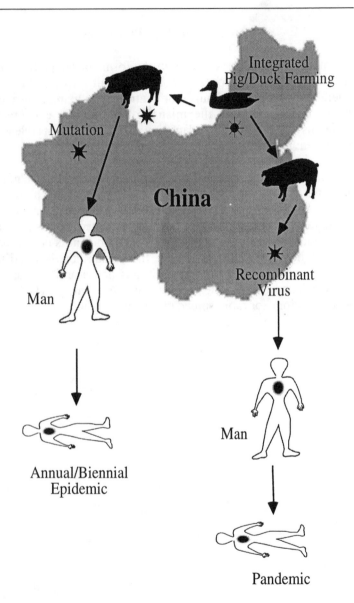

Figure 1.2. Influenza Origin and Spread.

The less serious forms of influenza common in annual or biennial epidemics result from totally different processes of natural antigenic change. The organisms undergo relatively small variations in their protein structures. This process is illustrated in Figure 1.3. These new differences are sufficient to protect them from existing antibodies existing in the human population. Consequently, we have frequent outbreaks of new serologic strains.

Figure 1.3. Antigenic change.
* *

A totally new process may be starting in late 1997. Health officials in the People's Republic of China have reported the first case ever recorded of direct bird to human transmission of a new strain of avian influenza virus. It has been confirmed as a new mutant type designated H5N1 by WHO and CDC laboratories. However, proof of the epidemiologic process involved has not yet been reported in peer reviewed literature. The investigators have not yet drawn conclusions from the very limited information available.

Media hype may be causing panic without a basis. WHO and CDC scientists are attempting to determine if the new strain should be included in the 1998 flu vaccine. Partly in response to public fears, Hong Kong authorities have ordered the destruction of over a million chickens as an attempt to limit spread. In December, 1997, Hong Kong health authorities said that one of the early reported deaths was actually due to Reye's Syndrome.

This one will be interesting to watch. Is it an isolated incident or the beginning of a new pandemic?

Another example of natural processes is the development of antibiotic resistance by many bacteria. Here we find a perfect example of adaptation to environmental changes and survival of the fittest - those organisms which are not affected by the antibiotic.

If the adaptation to the antibiotic involves genetic change, it can spread to other species by natural recombination of DNA. Likewise, a gene for resistance to the antibiotic it produces can be transferred to other bacteria from the producer. This is illustrated in Figure 1.4.

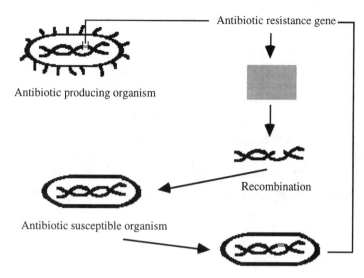

Figure 1.4. DNA recombination.

* *

When such changes occur, man's defensive weapons are rendered harmless and a disease which was once controlled breaks out anew. The process is not limited to a single gene. Multidrug resistance can result from multiple recombinations. The early 1997 outbreak of Salmonellosis caused by *Salmonella typhimurum* serotype DT104, is a frightening instance of multidrug resistance development. The Genus *Salmonella* includes many species which produce intestinal infections ranging from very mild to fatal. *S. typhimurium* is definitely not one of the mild types. Many other problems will be described as we discuss specific diseases.

People Factors

Many of the new and emerging disease problems revolve around human behaviors. In fact, human behavior is often the weak link in the chain of disease control as illustrated here.

* *

1. **Disease Recognized**

2. **Epidemiology Established**

3. **Treatment Provided**

4. **Source Blocked**

5. **Human Behavior**

6. **Control**

* *

Rapid worldwide travel is sometimes a major factor. A person can become infected with an isolated disease found only in a single local area and within less than twenty-four hours be carrying it to the opposite side of the world. The problem involves not only traveling humans but also their goods of commerce. Transport of many items provides an easy method for relocation of insect vectors as well as the specific etiologic agents themselves.

Changes in the makeup and distribution of human societies are another major factor. Within only a few generations, the world has transformed from relatively isolated small rural populations, to massive crowding in high density life styles of cities. Figure 1.5 shows how the U.S. population density has increased from around 26 to almost 90 people per square mile during the Twentieth Century. Such changes, of course, bring more and more people into close contact with each other, thereby providing greater opportunity for diseases to spread. Not all such population changes have direct human to human effects. Some may involve relationships with other organisms such as rats, which often become a major factor in lower socioeconomic areas of overcrowded cities.

* *

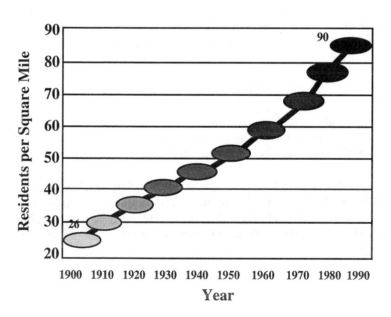

Figure 1.5. Population Density in U.S. Project to 2000 at 80-90 rate. Source: U.S. Census Data.

The food supply can be another source of problems. In the not too distant past most food was produced and consumed within a very small limited geographic area. Such is no longer the case.

The food we eat today may have left the other side of the world only yesterday or last week. Thus, food borne infectious agents have a rapid opportunity to spread. Good examples of such problems include the "Mad Cow Disease" and hamburger meat contaminated by particularly virulent strains of *Escherichia coli.*

Additional dangers are inherent when a food crosses international borders with the chain of public health control compromised. The March, 1997, outbreak of hepatitis A, from Mexican strawberries clearly shows the need for more stringent monitoring on both sides of a border. Later in 1997, several outbreaks of cyclosporal diarrhea in the U.S. were traced to contaminated raspberries from Guatemala. Repeated contamination caused the USDA to ban further imports until the problem is controlled.

Ecological Changes

Ecological changes almost immediately follow land use changes. While massive destruction of rain forests is the most dramatic example, other changes can result in disease problems.

Something as simple as a rancher converting grazing land to grain production can enhance the spread of a disease which has a lower animal natural reservoir. The recent increase in Argentine hemorrhagic fever resulted from such a seemingly simple change. (Figure 1.6)

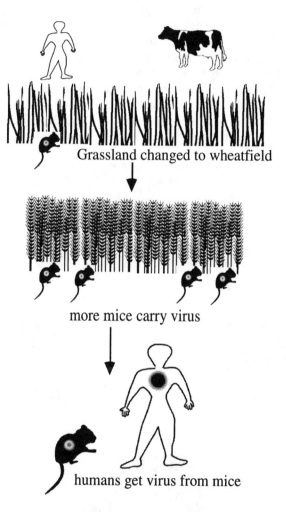

Grassland changed to wheatfield

more mice carry virus

humans get virus from mice

Figure 1.6. Junin virus increase from conversion of grazing land to grain production results in increase in Argentine hemorrhagic fever.

Artificial changes in the ecology of normal natural food chains introduce possibilities for spreading diseases from one species to another. Many biologists are expressing concerns about a currently developing practice of recycling chicken and cattle manure in the feed of the other species as illustrated in the cycle shown in Figure 1.7. Farmers utilizing the practice defend it by saying there have been no proven disease outbreaks as a result (in late 1997). While their statements are true, this author sides with those who view the practice as trouble being invited to happen.

* *

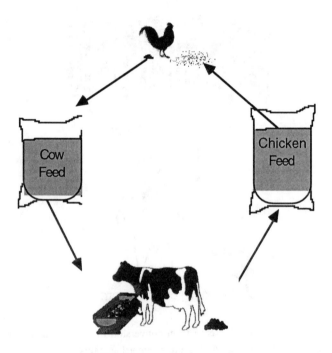

Figure 1.7. Manure/Feed Cycle

Pollution Problems

Closely related to increasing population pressures and ecological changes are resulting human waste pollution problems. Prime examples are areas with rapidly increasing populations such as the Texas Gulf Coast. According to the Texas Natural Resource Conservation Commission (1995), the state had 1,970 square miles of shellfish harvesting waters. Harvesting was restricted or prohibited in over 600 square miles. Only conditional approval was granted in 166 square miles. The underlying cause in all cases was probable human waste contamination as evidenced by the presence of fecal coliform bacteria.

A New Means Of Spread

This one couldn't happen. It is too ridiculous to even consider. So was the World Trade Center bombing. So was the Murrah Building in Oklahoma City. But, in a world with more than its share of lunatic terrorists, they happened. This one can, too.

SCENE I: An indoor sports stadium crowded with 60,000 fans.

Scene II: A large government building during working hours.

Scene III: A large movie theater showing the latest hit to a standing room only crowd.

At any location such as these, a terrorist using what looks like a small vial of aerosol nasal spray is not likely to draw much attention. A few short squirts fills the air handling system with billions of pathogens causing one of the more uncommon new diseases.

Just as an army would do before using a biological warfare weapon, the perpetrator has previously immunized himself against the disease. Careful selection of the pathogen to be used would provide a high or low mortality rate as desired.

Kaufmann *et al* (1997) developed computer models to predict and assess the cost of three different bioterrorism attacks. Even in one with a high morbidity, but low mortality rate, the economic cost is staggering. Their study also predicted how the results of the attack could be ameliorated by rapid medical response.

Dr. Philip Russell (1997) of Johns Hopkins University commented on the Kaufmann study. He thinks that civilian medicine is poorly prepared to provide the intervention that would be needed if the terrorist uses an uncommon disease. One of Russell's major concerns is that public health response to such an emergency is too widely dispersed among too many local, state, and federal agencies. Another is that the medical establishment has problems in appropriately dealing with unfamiliar diseases. The validity of his concern on this subject is clearly illustrated by examples of misdiagnosis and improper treatment cited elsewhere in this book.

Both Kaufmann *et al* and Russell express concern about the cost and other problems associated with proper preparation of the medical profession to deal with bioterrorism. Again, this raises questions of how much of our national resources we are willing to devote to such preparation.

Anyone who believes bioterrorism could not happen needs a thinking adjustment hour. It already has - fortunately, on a small scale.

Kolavie *et al* (1997) described an outbreak of diarrheal illness resulting from contamination of hospital employees' food in 1996 by a rare strain of *Shigella dysenterae*. The bacteria isolated from the infections was identical to a reference strain maintained in the hospital lab. Further investigation showed some of the lab culture to be missing. Deliberate contamination was suspected.

The story reached a climax in late August, 1997, when a Dallas County, Texas grand jury indicted a former hospital employee on several charges. Prosecutors allege that she had deliberately contaminated doughnuts and muffins in the employees break room as a means of revenge against a former boyfriend with whom she had disagreements. Yes, he suffered, but so did 11 other innocent people.

Let's conclude this discussion with one final disquieting thought. In reviewing proposals for preparing to meet the threat of biological terrorism, Dr. Jeffrey Simon (1997) stated, " ...we are today with respect to BW terrorism where we were nearly 30 years ago with respect to conventional terrorism." Preparation of an infective biological agent is considerably easier, less risky, and less expensive than making a bomb. It can be done even by a person with limited training in microbiology. Hopefully, if such a person tries it, his lack of experience will result in self-elimination before the preparation is released on the world.

A New Way To Get Infected

New inventions and processes are usually accompanied by new words to describe them. Let's take a moment to examine the language before we look at a unique new way to get an infection.

Zoonosis are diseases which are naturally communicable to man from lower animals. The prefix "xeno-" refers to foreign or unusual material or circumstance. Xenozoonosis refers to new diseases resulting from xenografts which are surgical grafts or transplants of tissue from one species into another. At this point, little imagination is required to predict where this section is headed.

Meslin (1997) summarized concerns of the World Health Organization about the potential of new Zoonosis in humans resulting from surgical or injectable use of lower animal tissues. He points out that all transplant procedures including allografts (human to human) carry a risk of transmitting a disease which is undetected in the donor. The WHO predicts a near-term dramatic increase in the number of xenotransplants and is developing guidelines to assure that donor tissues are free of known infectious agents. The subject received major attention at the recent (1996) First International Congress on Emerging Zoonoses.

In his 1997 summary, Meslin noted that transplant recipients are at special risk to develop infections because their immune systems are usually suppressed to prevent rejection of the donor tissue. Once the disease is established in the xenotransplant patient, it could spread rapidly through the human population because the degree of natural immunity to a new disease is extremely low, if it exists at all.

Unfortunately, the preventive screening procedures being developed by the WHO might give a false sense of security. What will happen if the xenozoonosis is one not resulting from a living detectable microorganism, but like the Mad Cow Disease, is caused by a protein or other less-than-life chemical structure?

Physician Errors

A major problem in dealing with new and reemerging diseases is errors in diagnosis by the attending physician. In all fairness to the doctors, we must consider that recognizing and correctly naming a condition rarely, if ever, seen before is difficult. However, early accurate diagnosis is vital for both welfare of the patient and control of potential disease spread.

An example of the problem appears in a study of murine typhus in Texas between 1979 and 1987. Of 96 confirmed cases, the correct diagnosis was initially missed in 23. The original diagnosis in these 23 included:

1. Avian chlamydiosis
2. Babesiosis
3. Brucellosis
4. Leptospirosis
5. Lyme borreliosis
6. Malaria
7. Q fever
8. Rat bite fever
9. Relapsing fever
10. Rocky Mountain spotted fever
11. Salmonellosis
12. Tularemia
13. Zoonotic epidemic typhus

In a similar study of 200 brucellosis cases, 98 were misdiagnosed initially as one of these:

1. Blastomycosis
2. Histoplasmosis
3. Listeriosis
4. Lyme borreliosis
5. Q fever
6. Rat bite fever
7. Salmonellosis
8. Toxoplasmosis
9. Trichinellosis
10. Viral hepatitis A

These studies were done by Carter *et al* (1997) in evaluating what is being called "Knowledge-Based Patient Screening" as a diagnostic aid for physicians. The process utilizes a computerized "decision support system" which is essentially a database of factors related to different diseases. The factors include, but are not limited to clinical history, diagnostic tests used and their results, etiology, vectors, invertebrate hosts, bibliographic citations, etc. Patient factors incorporated include occupation, travel and food consumption history, unusual dietary practices, animal and insect exposure, symptoms, etc.

The investigators note that the use of such a system could have shortened the time for reaching an accurate diagnosis and saved the patient much discomfort and money wasted on inappropriate procedures.

This cited research report raised some grave, almost unbelieving concerns when I first read it. They do not relate to the quality of the investigation or the report. Dr. Craig Carter and his colleagues appear to have done a thorough job. The concerns do relate to the necessity for such a project. Perhaps this author is living in the past when physicians took time to become acquainted with their patients and were competent to take a thorough history without computer prompting. That was in the dark ages of medicine when patients were people, not just numbers shuffled around in HMO's.

If technology such as described here is needed by modern doctors to speed up diagnosis, it should be used because a few days can seriously affect our ability to control a budding epidemic

New Vectors

Well, they are really not new themselves, but they are new in some places. They can transmit previously unknown diseases in those places.

In times long past, western man marveled at the exotic diseases of the tropics and the far east and was thankful that he did not have to worry about them. Today, that is changing. Modern transportation and expanded trade make it easy for formerly isolated insect vectors to hitch a ride to far away places.

The recent introduction of the Asian Tiger Mosquito (ATM) to the United States and Brazil as illustrated in Figure 1.8 provides the means for transmission of new diseases. Unfortunately, the ATM, now becoming well established in Texas and spreading to other southern states, is also capable of transmitting our own mosquito borne infections. Brazil is facing a similar threat. The more vectors it has, the harder a disease is to control.

* *

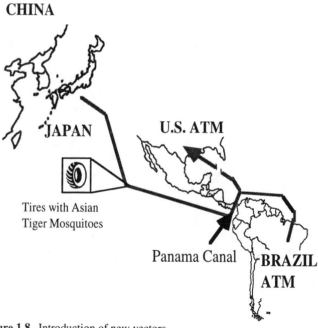

Figure 1.8. Introduction of new vectors.

Combined Problems

A frightening example of how an uncommon disease can spread throughout the world almost overnight was recently reported in detail by a public health investigation team (Hedberg, 1992). Shigellosis is a general name given to several varieties of moderate to severe diarrhea caused by members of the genus *Shigella*. In this case, the causative organism was *Shigilla sonnei* which causes a relatively mild, but uncomfortable form of the disease. Shigellosis is not technically considered an emerging disease because it has been present for centuries. However, incidents of *Shigella* infections are increasing at a rapid rate and public health officials are concerned. Be that as it may, the outbreak described clearly illustrates how several different factors can be involved in the spread of a disease. They would be equally applicable to a new or reemerging one.

In this instance the outbreak was associated with consumption of cold sandwiches served on commercial airline flights originating in Minneapolis - St. Paul, Minnesota. The food was hand prepared in the airline's flight kitchen and served on flights originating from that airport. This classic index outbreak initially came to the attention of public health authorities because it involved a professional football team along with other passengers. Almost one-third of the football team and many other passengers became ill with symptoms of Shigellosis from twelve to ninety-six hours following consumption of the food. Antibody studies and serotyping of the bacteria isolated from stool specimens indicated a common point of origin. Before the outbreak was contained a large number of passengers on other flights suffered the same illness. In all, within a month cases had been traced to twenty-four states, the District of Columbia, and four other countries. At least thirteen flights served the contaminated food.

The affected passengers were questioned and it became apparent that a common factor was in-flight consumption of cold foods such as sandwiches that were prepared by hand in the airline's flight kitchen. The kitchen in question had modern state of the art facilities, but had been cited for deficiencies related to handling food. These included cold items stored above 4°C and surfaces of equipment and utensils inadequately cleaned and sanitized. An additional citation had been issued for some employees who were observed failing to wash their hand when returning to the kitchen from the bathroom.

Eight of 94 food handlers told of having had symptoms of diarrhea preceding the outbreak. Five had positive antibody titers for *S. sonnei*. Two of these were on work schedules which involved preparation of food for the flights in question. The public health team investigating the outbreak concluded that the major cause was failure of the airline to adequately train and supervise the handlers. Other factors possibly contributed.

It is interesting to note that the *S. sonnei* serotype was identical to that found in earlier cases of Shigellosis occurring in Minneapolis residents over a period of months before the outbreak,. The inevitable conclusion to be drawn is that isolated endemic infections became concentrated in a central point which served for rapid worldwide dispersal. Thus, the example provides a clear study of how travel, food source, and human behavior function together to start an epidemic.

Climate Factors

One does not need a college degree in biology or meteorology to understand that unusual climate changes can affect disease incidence, especially diseases spread by insect vectors. However, when warming, drought, or excessive rainfall enable an insect to change its normal geographic range, the distribution of any diseases carried by that insect will also change. Most such climate changes are slow and gradual, sometimes extending over periods of hundreds of years as was the case during the age of the great glaciers. Other changes involve a very short period of time and are much more dramatic.

One of the most common examples of regular oscillations in world climate patterns is that of El Niño episodes. El Niño is a complex climate change resulting in unusually intense wet periods affecting the countries and continents bordering the Pacific and Indian Oceans. The other extreme is less well known and referred to as La Niña. Disruptions of weather patterns become more pronounced during a Southern oscillation of El Niño referred to as Enso. Enso brought drought and famine to India and floods to Australia. Nicholls (1993) reviewed the effects of Enso on a number of viral diseases. He found evidence that the climate extremes were a major factor in habitat changes of several different species of mosquitoes and consequently, the viruses they carry. Nicholls showed that the disease changes involved Australian encephalitis, Eastern Equine encephalitis, Nile fever, and Japanese encephalitis. A sharp increase in the number of malaria cases in South America was also associated with the heavy rains accompanying Enso. Nicholls' views suggests that some of the increased vector borne disease incidents could be prevented by increasing mosquito control procedures at the first sign of El Niño changes.

A more recent example of El Niño problems was the hurricane which struck Acupulco in the fall of 1997. Heavy rains caused flood waters to become contaminated with sewage. Mexican health authorities were hard pressed to prevent a cholera epidemic.

Changing Prevention Programs

Reduction or other changes in public health disease prevention programs often contribute to the reemergence of a disease. Sometimes the reduced use of preventive measures is not the fault of public health authorities. The recent increase in the number of polio cases is quite simply the result of the failure of some parents to have their children vaccinated. Parents who were born after the mid-1950's have no way of knowing the horror of the polio epidemics which occurred prior to that time. Those who did experience that terrible disease and know the thumping wheeze of an iron lung encasing its tiny patient were anxious to have their children protected. Now, polio seems to be of only academic interest and many parents neglect vaccination. The disease is increasing.

Almost unbelievably, prevention is not a high priority item in the budgets of many developing countries. As described in our review of malaria, political leaders simply accept the age-old fact of high infant mortality and frequent disease epidemics. Hunger is more likely to create political unrest than is lack of infection control where disease is considered the normal way of life.

Section II
Frightening Infections

The Outbreaks, Epidemics,
and Pandemics

* *

*Some diseases discussed in this section are known by different names,
both popular and scientific. Some are grouped together because of
close similarities. To make referencing easier, each subject begins
with a list of its names and etiologic agent.*

* *

Avian Influenza H5N1

Avian influenza   Influenza virus H5N1
Bird flu

◆ ◆

"Watch out! Stay tuned for the latest on the bird flu."

Unfortunately, this one is tailor-made for media hype. At the end of 1997, health authorities do not know whether we are facing a new type of flu pandemic or simply dealing with an isolated mutant and public panic created by irresponsible reporting.

The virus strain serotyped H5N1 was isolated in Hong Kong in the fall of 1997. It is thought to be a mutant of a variety of influenza virus previously found only in chickens or other birds. Mutational changes enabled the virus to be transferred directly from birds to humans. Human to human transmission had not been confirmed at the year's end, but investigators thought it possible. Actually, only 12 cases with 5 deaths had been confirmed at the end of December.

Representatives of various health organizations, including WHO and CDC, met in Hong Kong in December to determine if H5N1 should be included in the 1998 flu vaccine. A conclusion had not been announced at press time for this book.

A massive slaughter of over a million chickens, geese, and ducks was ordered by Hong Kong authorities in mid-December in an attempt to eliminate the reservoir and public panic.

At the end of December the UN was attempting to determine the truth about reports of large numbers of "chicken flu" cases occurring in mainland China as early as March, 1997. Why the question and delay? The answer is simple and emphasizes the importance of international cooperation in epidemic prevention. The People's Republic of China is not a member of OEI, and therefore, under no obligation to report.

The severity of H5N1 flu had not been determined by year's end. Did the few hospitalized cases represent the norm of an extremely virulent virus, or were they a few exceptions with perhaps thousands of other cases so mild they were not seen by physicians?

You will find reliable sources of current updates on the situation at the EID and ProMED web sites. Question the reliability of commercial sites that look like flashing carnival lights.

BSE: The Mad Cow Disease Group

Bovine Spongiform Encephalopathy (BSE)   Prion(?)
Creutzfeldt-Jacob Disease (CJD)
Mad Cow Disease
Transmissible Spongiform Encephalopathy (TSE)

◆ ◆

While not entirely accurate, "Mad Cow Disease" is probably an easy way to describe a group of related conditions which have resulted in alphabetic madness in their designations. Technically these diseases are classified as TSE which stands for Transmissible Spongiform Encephalopathy. BSE, Bovine Spongiform Encephalopathy, is the most common form from which the name "Mad Cow Disease" has been derived. A similar human condition is known as Creutzfeldt-Jacob Disease, CJD. Recently, an apparently new one has appeared. It is called V-CJD which stands for variant Creutzfeldt-Jacob Disease. This is by no means all, but it should suffice for the moment.

The specific cause of these diseases is not well established, but all the evidence points to a prion of the type described in the first section of this book.

Some of the conditions have been around for a long time, but were considered rare as in the case of CJD. Other related neurological conditions such as scrapie in sheep have been well known. Similar conditions have occurred from time to time in other animals including mink, mule deer, and elk. More recently, the World Health Organization has reported cases in domestic cats, mostly in the United Kingdom. The TSE's caught our full attention in 1986, with a major outbreak of BSE in England. By 1995, over 150,000 cases had been confirmed in cattle in the United Kingdom and the disease had spread to ten other European countries. Its sudden appearance in native herds in these countries pointed toward a common source. In all cases, the animals had consumed cattle feed imported from England. All of this feed contained processed livestock proteins.

In humans, these related diseases result in a multitude of neurologic symptoms associated with breakdown of brain tissues. The first symptoms are usually behavioral changes such as anxiety, depression, withdrawal, forgetfulness, and later dementia. These gradually increase in severity over a period of several weeks to a few months. Later, muscle dysfunction begins to occur as a result of damage to the cerebellum. Marked increases in the quantity of prion proteins occur, especially in the cerebellum. EEG patterns show characteristic changes. Post mortem examination of brain tissues reveals typical plaques associated with spongy edema.

The new variant of Creutzfeldt-Jacob Disease exhibits some distinctive brain lesions which are normally found only in persons suffering from Kuru disease. Previously, Kuru has been found only in a few tribes which practice cannibalism in Papua, New Guinea.

Still another new CJD variant may be appearing in the United States in late 1997. Dr. Joseph Berger, Jr., head of the neurology department at the University of Kentucky, and his associates have recently reported a possible relation involving squirrel brains as a source of CJD (Berger, Jr. *et al*, 1997).

Apparently in some areas of Tennessee and Kentucky where small game is hunted for food, some individuals consider raw squirrel brains a delicacy to accompany the otherwise cooked meal. Dr. Berger and his colleagues note that a common factor in human CJD in that area is such consumption of squirrel brains.

If what these researchers suspect is proven to be true, we shudder to think of the sensationalism an irresponsible popular press will create. The bottomless pit of yellow journalism will probably sink to a new low with the Mad or Crazy Squirrel Disease.

The discovery of TSE in squirrels should be considered in the context of spongiform encephalopathies known to exist in many animal species as early as the 1980's.

Prevention Strategies

Since there is no effective treatment for any of these disease, the only hope for control is prevention. To this end, the WHO has convened several special conferences during the years 1995 to 1997. Initial attempts at control included a ban on the use of bovine tissues in livestock feeds. This undoubtedly was a major factor in the decline of BSE in England during the late 1980's. The disease has by no means been eliminated, with new cases still being reported in both livestock and humans in 1997. In April, 1996, WHO convened a joint conference with the U.N. Food and Agriculture Organization (FAO) and Office International des Epizooties (OIE), to formalize a recommendation for control of the BSE diseases. Here are the major areas covered by the recommendation:

1. No part or product of any animal which has shown signs of a TSE should enter either a human or animal food chain.

2. All countries should establish continuous surveillance and compulsory notification of all BSE cases.

3. Tissues that are likely to contain the BSE agent should not enter the food chain.

4. All countries should ban the use of any ruminant tissues in ruminant feed.

5. Medicinal products and devices derived from bovine tissues must be processed in a way that reduce the risk of infection, recognizing that physical and chemical agents effective against most bacteria and viruses may be ineffective against the BSE agent.

6. Milk and milk products, tallow, and gelatin were granted exceptions from the regulations because there is no evidence of BSE transmission through them.

7. All countries should promote research on TSE's with emphasis on rapid diagnosis, agent characterization, and epidemiology of both human and animal cases.

Unfortunately, one must remember that regardless of the merit of the recommendations of a U.N. Consultation, the organization has neither the authority nor means for enforcement.

In late 1997, medical researchers began expressing concern about the possibility of spreading V-CJD by organ transplants. One question involved the possibility that corneas might harbor prions if the deceased donor had a latent infection. The question is not yet answered.

Bunyaviruses : Sometimes The Answer Is "No"

Neural Tube Defects   Bunyavirus
                                                                 Cache Valley Virus

◆ ◆

When we form an hypothesis to answer a scientific question, we naturally hope our idea is correct. Alas, such is not always the case, and the experimental evidence says plainly and bluntly, "You are WRONG!" Any student who has ever suffered such ego-shattering experience with a science fair project can be consoled by the fact that it happens to professional scientists, too. It is important to remember that knowing what is not the answer is often the first necessary step to finding the truth.

Such was the experience of epidemiologists studying an unusually high incidence of brain defects of newborn infants in South Texas in 1990-1991. One of the early theories of the cause was finally disproved when all the bits and pieces of evidence were placed in the puzzle several years later (Edwards and Hendricks, 1997).

A little background information will help explain why the investigators adopted their original hypothesis. People have been hanged on far less circumstantial evidence.

Physicians use the term, "neural tube defects," to classify three major types of birth defects involving the formation of the central nervous system. The most serious of these is anencephaly, a condition in which the brain fails to form and the infant is stillborn or dies soon after birth. Spina bifida is a condition in which the spinal cord is not properly covered. It is often surgically correctable. Encephaloceles are skull openings through which meninges covered brain tissue extends to the outside. Small ones can be surgically closed with varying degrees of residual neurologic damage.

The Cache Valley Virus (CVV) is a member of the bunyavirus group which is common in North America. It has long been recognized as an insect vectored pathogen of ruminants in which infection of pregnant females results in severe brain and musculoskeletal defects of the offspring. Related bunyaviruses were known to cause similar problems in experimentally infected animals with transmission by *Aedes* species mosquitoes as early as 1972 (Patawatana *et al*).

A sudden dramatic increase in neural tube defects, especially anencephaly, occurred in Brownsville, Texas in 1990 and continued through 1991. Prior to that time the incidence of neural tube defects in South Texas was not appreciably higher than in the rest of the United States. A glance at Figure 2.1 will quickly reveal the reason for concern.

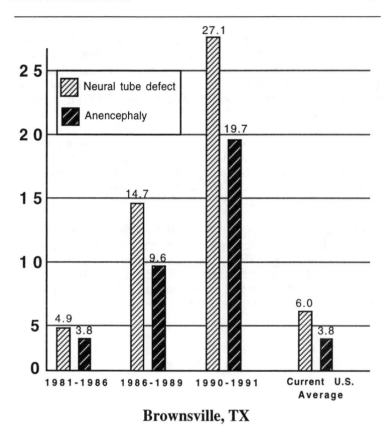

Brownsville, TX

Figure 2.1 - Neural tube defects in Brownsville, TX, 1981-1991.

A search began for possible causes or events that might be related. One of the few that turned up was a severe epidemic of CVV neural tube defects of newborn lambs in West Texas that had started three years earlier. In the absence of other factors, the question quickly became one of whether the CVV virus could cross over to humans.

CVV infections of ruminants and other animals are known to induce antibody production in the mother's blood. Consequently, sera from 74 women who had given birth to neural tube defect babies during the outbreak was analyzed for antibodies. None were found in tests conducted from 1993 to 1995.

Edwards and Hendricks (1997) noted that while the test results seem to rule out CVV etiology in the South Texas outbreak, they do not rule out the possibility that other bunyaviruses might have been involved. In the meantime, studies continue with respect to dietary folic acid levels and environmental pollutants which are sometimes associated with neural tube defects.

Chlamydial Infections

Lymphogranuloma venereum   *Chlamydia trachorralis*
Pelvic Inflammatory Disease
♦ ♦

Infections caused by *Chlamydia trachorralis* and often associated PID (Pelvic Inflammatory Disease) are certainly not new, but they are emerging as a major problem. The CDC estimates about four million new cases a year in the United States. PID is now considered a major cause of infertility in women. One strain of the Chlamydial organism is now recognized as the etiologic agent of lymphogranuloma venereum, long known as a rare sexually transmitted disease, particularly in the tropical South Pacific.

Transmission of chlamydial infections is by vaginal, anal, or oral sexual contact. In newborn infants which are infected by the mother during delivery, the organism may cause eye infections and pneumonia.

Onset of symptoms occurs within 1 to 3 weeks of exposure. In both sexes they include pain during urination. Females may experience vaginal discharge. The initial symptoms are often very mild. In fact, approximately one-half of the women and one-fourth of the men infected have no initial symptoms. A situation such as this gives complications a chance to develop without warning or a possibility for early preventative treatment.

In males, the infection may result in inflammation of the scrotal organs, resulting in scarring and infertility. The most serious complication in females is PID which spreads into the Fallopian tubes, resulting in infertility or ectopic pregnancy.

In both sexes, chlamydia can cause inflammation of the rectum or throat.

Diagnosis and control are complicated by the fact that chlamydia are difficult to grow for identification by standard laboratory procedures. Recently developed procedures for detection by bacterial protein staining are more rapid and less expensive, although not as accurate.

Another complication in control is that chlamydial infections often occur along with gonorrhea which presents definitive symptoms that may mask the chlamydia. Since the chlamydia are not sensitive to penicillin and some other antibiotics often used to treat gonorrhea, they often persist after the gonorrhea is cured.

This is another disease which human behavior makes difficult to control. Unprotected sex is a particular problem because the disease can be transmitted even from subclinical cases. Some health authorities are recommending that all persons who have more than one sex partner should be tested to help break the chain of transmission. This recommendation seems especially important for women under age 25 and at the first diagnosis of pregnancy.

Cholera

Cholera *Vibrio cholera*
◆ ◆

In his exhaustive textbook, **Bacterial and Mycotic Infections of Man**, Rene J. Dubose (1952) seemed pleased to state that there had been no cases of cholera in the Americas for over fifty years. Freedom from the disease continued for almost forty more years until an outbreak occurred in Peru in 1991. Since that time, over a million cases of cholera have been reported in South and Central America.

The disease, caused by *Vibrio cholerae*, was recognized long before Robert Koch in 1883 discovered and described the organism. The first clue that it was spread by contaminated water was provided by Snow (1854) in an epidemic in London. A major outbreak in Hamburg, Germany in 1892 was traced to a contaminated water supply. We recognize today that spread of the disease is by means of water and food contaminated with human excreta.

Following ingestion of the contaminated food or water, the bacteria multiply rapidly in the intestines. As they grow, toxins are produced in large quantities and the lining of the intestine responds by attempting to wash away the irritants with a profuse outpouring of fluid. The result, of course, is severe diarrhea followed by life threatening dehydration. The severity of the diarrhea and quantity of fluid produced is attested by loss of normal fecal characteristics of the stools which are often described as appearing like rice water. Shock is a common result of the dehydration. In severe cases which involve a large contamination, death may occur within a few hours from the onset of symptoms. In more prolonged cases the lining of the intestine may be sloughed off with severe bleeding. If the patient recovers, there will be some future immunity.

As a result of some of the early massive epidemics being related to contaminated water, other possible sources of spread are frequently overlooked. Actually, the disease can be spread by flies and direct contact as well as contaminated water and food. Sometimes a single source can be pinpointed as was the case in Egypt in 1947 when an epidemic occurred from contaminated dates.

At this time we are not certain why cholera has reappeared in Latin America and spread with such rapidity. One study (Tauxe *et al*, 1995) points to at least one factor being increasing urbanization with many people living in substandard dwellings with inadequate sanitation.

The 1991 outbreak in Peru was the first South American epidemic to occur in the twentieth century. Over a half million cases with 4700 fatalities occurred as the disease spread through nineteen countries. Swerdlow *et al* (1992) carried out an extensive study of the epidemic that began in Trujillo, Peru in January, 1991. Part of the title of their study was "...lessons for a continent at risk." Truer words were never written!

The authors of this study concluded that the epidemic was primarily water-borne. Their findings would make a classic case for an epidemiology textbook. Unchlorinated water supply, sewage contamination, human wastes used as fertilizer, dipping hands into drinking water storage vessels, food of unknown origin--all the no no's were in place. Figure 2.2 graphically illustrates the consequences. (The totals are more than 100 per cent because many of the victims exposed themselves to more than a single risk.)

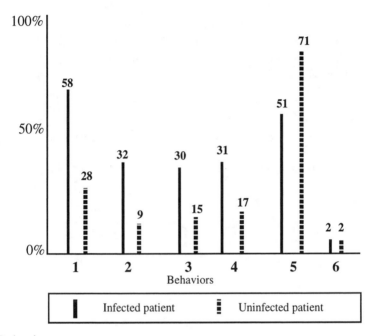

Behaviors:

1. Drank unboiled water.
2. Drank container-stored water into which hands had been introduced.
3. Went to a fiesta.
4. Ate cabbage.
5. Ate bananas.
6. Ate raw seafood.

Figure 2.2 - Exposure risk behaviors of 50 cholera patients within 3 days of onset of symptoms.

The hands in stored water factor is almost unbelievable to many people, but it is a major problem in undeveloped areas of the world. Deb *et al* (1986) showed that a dramatic reduction in disease transmission occurred in Calcutta, India when narrow-necked water storage containers were used to prevent contamination by hands.

The lessons of this case will be repeated. It is not a matter of IF; it is a matter of WHEN and WHERE. If you don't believe that, take a look at raw sewage contamination problems in Lake Houston, the source of a large part of that city's water supply.

Coccidioidomycosis

Coccidioidomycosis   *Coccidioides immitis*
San Joaquin Fever
Valley Fever

♦ ♦

The etiologic agent of Coccidioidomycosis is a fluffy cottony white fungus known as *Coccidioides immitis*. The infection produced by this organism actually functions as almost two separate diseases. The common initial form is a relatively benign, usually self limited respiratory infection. The second type is a progressive systemic disease involving lymph system spread which often results in death. The latter form is sometimes referred to as coccidioidal granuloma.

About two to four per cent of the victims of the respiratory form develop severe allergic hypersensitivity after five to fourteen days. The symptoms include a severe skin rash which lasts from one to four weeks. This form of the disease is often referred to as Valley Fever or San Joaquin Fever, named after the California locations where it was first observed.

Spread of *C. immitis* infections is ordinarily by dust borne spores. Other means, including man to man transmission directly, are possible. The disease was first described in Argentina in the late 1800's. Within a few years similar conditions were recognized in California, Arizona, and West Texas. Other cases have been reported from Italy, the Hawaiian Islands, Central America, and Southeastern Europe.

People who have lived most of their lives in the endemic areas of the Southwestern United States have a high level of antibodies to the organism. The acute infection occurs most frequently in newcomers to the area. Such data indicates that a large portion of the population may have subclinical infections sufficient to stimulate the immune system, but not to produce a recognizable disease. More recent studies such as those of Kushwaha *et al* (1996) following major outbreaks in South America indicated that the blood antibody level correlates with age. Higher immunity levels were found in older persons. Very young children showed low rates of antibody production.

Reemergence

During the early 1990's the incidence of coccidioidomycosis increased rapidly in California. Even though most cases were of the self limited respiratory variety it is estimated that direct and indirect cost, of the disease in Kern County alone have exceeded 66 million dollars since 1990 (Kirkland and Fierer, 1996). In their extensive review of the increased cases, these researchers concluded that major factors might be climatic and population changes. An additional factor which might be considered separately is the increased susceptibility of immunity compromised persons including AIDS patients.

Any condition which suppresses the normal functioning of the immune system makes the individual highly susceptible to coccidioidomycosis and a host of other infectious diseases. Artificial immune suppression is a problem experienced by many organ transplant patients. Natural suppression occurs following other pathologic conditions, not the least of which is AIDS. A number of researchers (Ampel, 1996; Hood and Denning, 1996; Doty, 1996) have done extensive studies which show a high incidence and apparent ease of infection in patients whose immune systems are functioning at a low level as a result of AIDS. Life threatening forms of coccidioidomycosis are much more common in AIDS patients than in other populations. It has also been noted that in persons whose immune systems are not functioning at a normal level, multiple fungal infections may occur at the same time. Careful diagnosis is required to select appropriate treatments to cover all the diseases which might be present (Doty, 1996).

The geographic distribution of the new cases of coccidioidomycosis appears to be the same as the historic endemic areas. There are simply many more cases.

Cryptosporidiosis

Cryptosporidiosis   *Cryptosporidium parvum*
◆ ◆

Cryptosporidiosis is an infectious disease characterized by moderate to severe diarrhea which may last over two weeks. It is caused by a protozoan, *Cryptosporidium parvum.*

The disease is by no means new, having been first discovered in mice in 1907. The infections caused by *C. parvum* and related species were considered to be veterinary diseases until 1976, when the first human case was described by Nime *et al.* During the next six years, only seven additional human cases were reported. By the mid-1990's cryptosporidiosis was threatening to become a widespread severe problem.

Human symptoms are a persistent watery diarrhea usually accompanied by severe abdominal cramping. About half the victims also experience fever and vomiting. Weight loss of ten pounds or more is not uncommon during the course of the infection. The disease does not become systemic, remaining limited to the lining of the intestine

Fortunately, cryptosporidiosis is self-limited because we have no really effective treatment. Only one known drug, paramomycin, produces any benefit, but it is by no means a cure. It does reduce the number of oocysts shed by the organism, thereby decreasing stool frequency and mass. Public health officials suspect that residual damage to the intestine lining might make the victim more susceptible to various bacterial infections in future years. At press time for this book, however, there is not yet any published data to support their theory, although studies are in progress.

Deaths from the infection have occurred primarily in immunocompromised patients such as AIDS victims. Other fatal outcomes have been reported in young children and persons already suffering various debilities.

During the infective process, our bodies apparently produce gamma globulin antibodies which persist after recovery. Studies based on the presence of these IgG antibodies to *C. parvum* in healthy persons indicate that the disease may have been more widespread than suspected in the past. Figure 2.3 compares the prevalence rate of antibodies in samplings from Brazil, China, and the United States.

* *

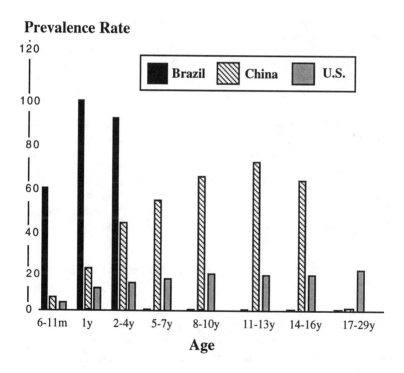

Figure 2.3 . Presence of antibodies to *Cryptosporidium* species by age in Brazil, China, and the United States.

Spread of cryptosporidiosis can be by a variety of the usual contaminated food and personal or fomite contact methods. Typical examples include apple cider (Millard *et al*, 1995), child care facilities (Cordell and Addiss, 1994) and hospitals (Neill *et al*, 1996). The most severe outbreaks have been water borne. A major problem with the disease is that *C. parvum* and other species of the genus are not susceptible to the levels of chlorine used in water supplies. Goldstein *et al* (1996) pointed out that outbreaks can occur from drinking water despite state of the art water treatment.

The apple cider outbreak of cryptosporidiosis documented by Millard *et al* (1994) is a classic example of modern epidemiological detective work. It is one of the very rare instances of transmission of the disease by contaminated food. As such, it raises a warning flag about possible future problems originating in a farm environment. It is the first point source outbreak studied.

The disease originated in two elementary schools in a farming region in central Maine. The school principals reported high absence rates among students who had attended an agriculture fair a week earlier. From the total of 759 fair attendants, 160 were diagnosed with cryptosporidiosis. One event of the fair was a demonstration of pressing apples to make fresh cider. Records revealed that 284 persons had attended the demonstration. The attendants included 154 of the initial 160 cases. All 154 cases drank some of the cider.

Over one-third of the primary cases transmitted the disease to other household members. Statistically, each primary case infected 1.3 other persons.

Apples for the afternoon demonstration had been gathered by students the previous day. Some were shaken from trees onto farm trucks; others were obtained from the ground under trees.

Cryptosporidium oocysts were found in leftover cider and on the press. They were also found in the feces of two calves on the farm from which the apples were obtained.

The fact that only two per cent of the cases of the disease occurred in persons who had not consumed the cider is additional evidence that it was the source.

Figure 2.4 summarizes the epidemiology of this outbreak.

The seriousness of the problem and urgency of need to develop new water treatment methods are exemplified by a massive outbreak which occurred in Milwaukee, Wisconsin in 1993. Before it was over, the epidemic affected over 400,000 people, which was more than half of those served by one water treatment plant. Although deaths occurred primarily in immunocompromised patients, many other persons suffered severely. Guerrant (1997) summarized some of the problems which included an infection duration of up to 55 days. The average number of watery diarrhea stools at the peak of the infection was 19 per day and weight losses were around ten pounds.

Have we been caught in a Star Trek time warp and gone back in time? The major help the state health department could give was to advise Milwaukee residents to boil their drinking water. Somehow, that does not seem in tune with modern biotechnology. Hopefully, waterworks researchers who are frantically working on the problem will soon develop some new methods of water flocculation and filtration which will eliminate cryptosporidia in the water supply.

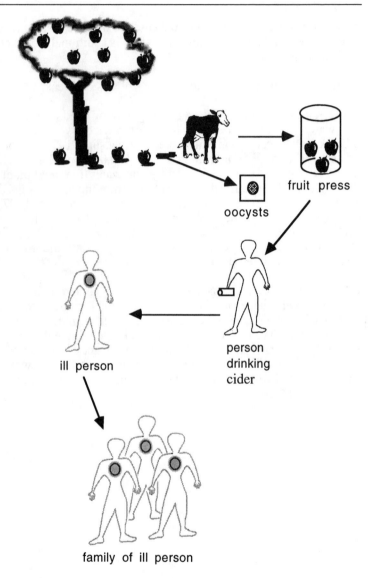

Figure 2.4. Cryptosporidiosis epidemiology.

Dengue and Dengue Hemorrhagic Fever

Break Bone Fever   Dengue Virus
Damn You Fever
Dengue Fever
Dengue Hemorrhagic Fever
Five Day Fever

♦ ♦

Some of the popular names given to Dengue Fever give a clue to
its characteristics. The disease has been called break bone fever,
dandy fever, five day fever, seven day fever, and perhaps most
popularly in the United States, Damn You Fever.

The disease was first described in Java in 1779. Within a few
years it was noticed in the United States and various other countries.
The Royal College of Physicians in London adopted the name in
1869. Severe epidemics have frequently occurred in many nations
including the United States, Greece, Japan, and Australia. Other
cases were found in Mexico during the first half of the twentieth
century. One of the worst recorded epidemics occurred in the
southern United States between 1922 and 1925 when it was
estimated that at least two million people contracted the disease.
Over half a million of these cases were reported in Texas.

The etiologic agent of the disease is a virus which is transmitted by mosquitoes of the genus *Aedes*. *A. aegypti* has been considered the major vector, perhaps because it is more widespread than *A. arbopictus* which some consider to actually be the primary vector. One of our concerns at the present time is that *A. arbopictus* has recently been introduced to the United States, It seems to be adapting well. An abundance of *A. Aegypti* of course already exists, particularly in the southern states. Numerous workers have reported the disease and isolation of its virus from monkeys. There is evidence that monkey to monkey or monkey to human transmission may occur. The monkeys which appear to be most often involved are classified in the genera *Cynomolgus* and *Ceropithecus*. It is interesting to note that these monkeys also harbor SIV (Simian immunodeficiency virus) which many now consider to be the source of the human immunodeficiency virus of AIDS (Morse *et al*, 1995).

The spread of Dengue Fever is becoming a major concern in many countries of South America as well as Southern Asia and the Pacific Islands.

E. coli Infections

E. coli gastroenteritis   *Escherichia coli* 0157:H7
Hemolytic uremic syndrome

◆◆

We used to think of *Escherichia coli* as a friendly harmless little inhabitant of our intestines. Our relationship with it went far beyond that--we recognized that it played a vital role in our ability to utilize some vitamins. It was easy to grow and considered harmless to handle in the laboratory; consequently, it provided us with much of our early knowledge of bacterial physiology. Because of its universal distribution in the human colon, we used its presence in food and water as evidence of fecal contamination. The genus name, *Escherichia*, was given in honor of the early German bacteriologist, Theodor Escherich; the species name, *coli,* of course refers to its habitat in the colon

The characteristics and value of the original *E. coli* remain, but a new and deadly variant of it has emerged. It is designated Serotype 0157:H7. In the digestive system, it causes mild to severe localized infections. When it escapes from the colon, the consequences are often fatal, especially when it invades the kidneys. There it causes an infection called hemolytic uremic syndrome which results in acute kidney failure, especially in children.

Altekruse *et al* (1997) at CDC estimate a minimum of 725,000 cases per year with about 200 deaths in the United States. The actual number of cases is probably far greater, because most milder ones are never seen and reported by a physician. The death rate also may be higher if we consider the long term complications of hemolytic uremic syndrome in children. Boyce *et al* (1995) place the death rate at approximately three per cent, but point out that approximately 12 per cent of the cases experience later terminal kidney disease, hypertension, and neurologic injury.

An early warning of impending problems was sounded by Riley *et al* (1983) who studied a limited outbreak in fast food hamburgers in 1982. At that time they described 0157:H7 as a "rare" serotype. Now, it is far from rare, and *E. coli* is rapidly becoming a part of our disease vocabulary. Ten years later an outbreak was traced to fresh apple cider (Besser *et al*, 1993). Since then, contaminated lettuce, raw milk, untreated water, and more ground beef sources have been implicated.

The mother of all contamination occurred in mid-1997 when Hudson foods recalled 25 million pounds of hamburger that had been distributed to food stores and some fast food operations. The USDA closed the Hudson plant that was the source. Shortly thereafter, the Hudson facility was acquired by another major food processor.

While the hamburger contamination received massive media attention and prompt government action, consumers were barely aware of other problems such as the earlier 1997 contamination in fresh alfalfa sprouts,which did not receive regulatory attention until weeks after it occurred. Why the discrepancy?

Several factors are involved. First is human behavior. We are far more likely to get excited about something wrong with our hamburger than we are about a problem in our alfalfa sprout salad. Hamburgers make headlines; alfalfa sprouts do not. Another factor is government responsibility. Meat is supervised by the well funded Department of Agriculture; alfalfa sprouts come under the jurisdiction of the FDA which has much more limited resources. By the time the FDA became aware of the problem, the fresh sprouts were gone. The meat was still in freezers all over the country.

The Outlook For Prevention

Can *E. coli* and other foodborne diseases be prevented? Probably, not completely. Bacteriologic analysis of food for the presence of pathogens is technically possible, but in mass production operations, it is not practical unless you are willing to pay twenty dollars a pound for hamburger. Checking each batch in an operation the size of Hudson Foods is simply not a viable option. The current spot-check procedures are going to miss some problems.

Some things can be done, but many of them are subject to public understanding of the problems.

At some point, the consumer must accept a degree of responsibility. Thorough cooking of hamburger or any other food will kill *E. coli* and most other bacterial as well as viral and protozoan pathogens. Fast food providers may need to apply less fast and more heat. If the meat is still pink, it has not been cooked enough to kill microorganisms that might be present.

Genital Herpes

Genital Herpes   Herpes Simplex Virus Type 2
◆ ◆

Genital herpes is a highly contagious genital disease caused by Type 2 Herpes Simplex virus (HSV). Type 1 HSV is the cause of common cold sores or fever blisters which usually occur around the mouth. Although it rarely happens, Type 1 can cause genital infections and Type 2 can cause cold sores.

While neither of the herpes diseases are new, the rapidly increasing incidence of genital herpes is creating new problems. Accurate data about the incidence of the disease is not available, but the USPHS estimates that about 30 million people are infected in the United States. At least 500,000 new cases probably occur each year. The statistics are given as estimates because many cases are not reported; others are so mild that they are never seen by a physician.

Symptoms of genital herpes vary greatly from one person to another. The initial infection is usually signaled by an itching sensation with burning pain in the legs, buttocks, and genital area. Females frequently report a vaginal discharge. A few days later lesions appear at the site of the infection. They sometimes also occur on the cervix in women and in the urethra of men. The lesions, which start as small red bumps, may progress to blister-like sores. These symptoms begin to disappear as the virus travels along sensory nerves to the spinal cord where it remains dormant for varying periods of time. Periodically thereafter, symptoms recur as the virus moves back to the site of the primary infection. Usually the recurrences are milder than the first one. Frequency of recurrent episodes varies greatly in different individuals and sometimes, even within the infected person.

Transmission of genital herpes is by sexual contact with an infected partner. Contrary to what some infected persons would like their friends to believe, there are few documented cases of transmission from toilet seats, hot tubs, etc. Most transmissions occur when the infected person is in an active state of the disease; however, the virus can sometimes reactivate and be shed near the original infection site without causing active symptoms. The unusual atypical site infections by both Type 1 and Type 2 viruses are probably associated with oral sexual contact.

A major concern in the epidemiology of genital herpes is transmission of the virus to the developing fetus of an infected mother. Approximately half of infected newborns either die or suffer permanent neurologic damage. Infection can occur at the time of birth if the mother is in an active stage or is shedding the virus without symptoms. Because of this danger, many obstetricians recommend Cesarean delivery. The risk to babies that become infected at the time of delivery can be reduced by prompt treatment with acyclovir.

Except in immunosuppressed persons, genital herpes is not considered a life threatening disease. Aside from the danger to newborns and discomfort experienced by the victim, most problems are psychological and social in nature. Many personal relationships suffer disruption of normal sexual functions. Problems in one area of sexual or social relationships frequently progress into other areas. The American Social Health Association (ASHA) provides literature about herpes from its Herpes Resource Center. Its website is listed in the appendix.

At the present time there is neither cure nor total prevention for genital herpes. The drug known as acyclovir will reduce the severity of symptoms, but does not eliminate the disease. Experimental vaccines are showing some promise in early testing, but are probably several years away from general use. The only prevention at present is avoidance of sexual intercourse during active outbreaks and the use of condoms at other times to avoid infection from asymptomatic shedding.

The incidence of at least half a million new cases of genital herpes each year in the U. S. has serious implications for the spread of other sexually transmitted diseases as a result of unprotected sexual intercourse.

Giardiasis

Giardiasis   *Giardia lamblia*
Giardial Diarrhea

◆ ◆

Giardiasis is actually neither a new nor reemerging disease. It has been around a long time, probably more so than we were aware. Today, it is becoming a more common problem.

The disease is an intestinal infection caused by a protozoan parasite, *Giardia lamblia*, which exists in two forms. The active stage is called a trophozoite. These attach to the lining of the small intestine where they feed and reproduce. When food passage pushes them into the colon where there is less water, they form a resistant survival form called a cyst. The cyst is excreted and remains dormant until ingested by the next victim and is activated by the stomach acid.

Many infections are very mild, causing only minor intestinal discomfort. Others are characterized by explosive gas, watery diarrhea, nausea, bloating, abdominal pain, and sometimes nausea. When present, these symptoms usually persist for a week to ten days.

Most cases of giardiasis are transmitted by ingestion of food and water contaminated with the cysts. Direct person-to person transmission often occurs in young children whose hands are contaminated. Anal sex has been implicated as another means of transmission.

We do not have accurate data about the extent of giardiasis worldwide because it is not a reportable disease in most countries. Aside from that, many cases are mild and never seen by a physician. Public health authorities estimate that around 20 per cent of the world population is infected.

The disease was formerly considered to be a problem primarily in tropical countries, but now it is recognized more often in temperate conditions. Many natural bodies of water, even in colder mountain areas of the United States, have been contaminated by human wastes, particularly in camping and recreational areas.

Another source appears to be nursery schools and day care centers for infants and young children. The U.S. Public Health Service estimates that about three times as many cases occur in children as in adults. Most of the cases in infants and toddlers probably result from direct fecal contamination by hand.

Under any conditions, spread of the disease is enhanced by the fact that even after recovery from an acute infection, cysts may remain dormant and be excreted from the intestine over a period of months or even years.

The USPHS has no active program to prevent the spread of giardiasis in the U.S., and because of its usual mildness, it receives little attention elsewhere. Most recommendations for control and prevention relate only to good personal hygiene and sanitation practices where the disease is known to exist. For example, day care staff should not change diapers in food preparation areas and should wash their hands after changing them. Toddlers should not share objects they might put in their mouths. (Have they seen any children of this age lately?) Where the water supply is contaminated it should be boiled, and uncooked fruits and vegetables grown in the area should be avoided.

The Hantaviruses

Epidemic Hemorrhagic Fever	Hantavirus
Hantavirus Pulmonary Syndrome	Andes Virus
Hemorrhagic Fever with Renal Syndrome	
Korean Hemorrhagic Fever	

◆◆

Biologists who consider viruses to be true forms of life classify one group in the genus *Hantavirus* of the family Bunyaviridae. At present, 14 different viruses are recognized in this group.

The hantaviruses cause two major disease entities. Hantavirus Pulmonary Syndrome (HPS) is a primary infection of the lungs. Its symptoms are largely the result of pulmonary capillary leakage. Hemorrhagic Fever with Renal Syndrome (HFRS) actually is the name now applied to some diseases previously known by other names such as Korean hemorrhagic fever and epidemic hemorrhagic fever. We are concerned with these diseases here because of their increased spread throughout the world and apparent changes in makeup of the viruses.

Rodents appear to be the primary natural host of the hantaviruses although other animal species have been implicated. Spread to humans is usually by inhalation of aerosols from rodent excreta. Few cases attributable to insect vectors have been reported. Direct human to human transmission was not thought to be a problem until recently when Wells *et al* (1997) reported a study of 20 cases in Argentina in which direct person-to-person transmission was strongly implicated. The virus strain responsible is probably a new one first isolated in 1995 and described by Lopez *et al* (1996). It is becoming known as the Andes Virus.

Symptoms and Disease Processes

One of the major problems in diagnosing Hanta virus infections is the non-specific nature of early symptoms. For example, the three most common initial symptoms are fever, chills, and myalgias (muscle pain and tenderness). Many patients also complain of headache, nausea, diarrhea, cough, and general malaise. This leads the physician to the logical conclusion that the patient could have almost anything, Around the seventh day, the situation suddenly changes.

Fluid moves from the blood to accumulate in heart and lung tissues. Blood chemistries and cell counts rapidly become abnormal and the patient may require respiratory assistance within 24 hours. If the disease progresses into the kidneys, renal hemorrhage may occur and kidney functions become abnormal or begin to shut down.

As is the case with other viral infections, no specific treatment is available. Supportive treatments are directed toward easing the victim's symptoms and gaining time for the immune system to do its job.

CDC statistics show a death rate in excess of fifty per cent for cases in the United States.

Epidemiology

Hanta virus infections are not new--at least, some of them are not. They have been known in Korea and other eastern countries for many years. They are relatively new to the western hemisphere and appear to be spreading. There is strong evidence that the original viruses are undergoing natural mutations or other changes resulting in new varieties in new places. The Andes Virus described above is considered by Lopez *et al* (1996) to be a variant of the Sin Nombre virus. Schmaljohn and Hjelle (1997) note that recent HPS cases in the southeastern United States have resulted from a newly identified clade of viruses that include the Andes strain. (OOPS... Another new word slipped in. "Clade" refers to a group of viruses that share a common ancestor.) Such relationships are being established by the use of DNA technology including PCR Procedures. Aside from academic interest, such knowledge is useful in tracing the spread of a disease outbreak.

Detective work that would make Sherlock Holmes and Paul Drake look like rank amateurs recently solved the mysteries of an outbreak of HPS in the Navajo Nation of the southwestern United States in 1993. Too many intriguing events would be lost if we try to summarize the story here, so we shall simply refer the reader to the whole story related by Karen Kreeger in **The Scientist** (1994, 1994a). Solving the problem indicates what can be accomplished with an unusually high degree of cooperation coupled with rapid response between many different government agencies and private individuals. It is a story of how things should work, but all too often, rarely do.

Legionnaires' Disease

Legionellosis   *Legionella pneumophila*
Legionnaires' Disease
Nosocomial Legionellosis
♦ ♦

Legionnaires' Disease or legionellosis, as it is sometimes called
is caused by *Legionella pneumophila*. It first gained public health
attention and received its name after a major outbreak at an
American Legion convention in 1976. Sporadic cases probably
existed earlier, but were not recognized and distinguished from
other pneumonias.

L. pneumophila does not grow on the ordinary media used for
bacterial identification. Hence, the presence of the organism is
easily missed if only routine procedures are used. Health officials
now recommend that when multiple cases of pneumonia-like
disease appear among people who experienced a similar
environmental situation, testing for *L. pneumophila* should be
done.

The organism typically multiplies in almost any natural or man-
made water source. The usual route of infection is inhalation of
it in aerosols created by the water. One of the most common
sources is air conditioning cooling towers. Others include showers,
humidifiers, and respiratory therapy equipment. Aspiration of
contaminated drinking water is also a possible source.

Increasing numbers of outbreaks in hospitals have caused the
disease to become a major nosocomial infection concern.
Nosocomial infections appear to be more severe than those from
other sources. At least, the death rate is higher. A 1996 CDC
study of over 3,500 cases found a mortality rate of 40 per cent in
nosocomial infections compared with 20 per cent in community
acquired cases. This does not imply that the nosocomial strains
are more virulent. Like most other etiologic agents of pneumonia,
L. pneumophila is an opportunist more likely to cause severe
problems in already debilitated victims than in previously healthy
ones.

The increasing frequency of nosocomial legionellosis has prompted the CDC to issue formal recommendations for its prevention (CDC, 1996). General recommendations are concerned with hospital staff education and surveillance and reporting.

The CDC document also includes recommendations pertaining to specific hospital equipment such as respiratory therapy apparatus, water faucets, etc. Major emphasis is placed on operation, construction, and location of cooling towers, the most common source of nosocomial as well as other infections.

Prevention of community outbreaks will entail expensive monitoring of air and water handling systems. Even with that in place, there will be practical limitations on its effectiveness. Legionnaires' disease might prove to be one we shall simply have to try to keep to a minimum and live with.

Malaria

Malaria   *Plasmodium falciparum*
Malaria Fever   *Plasmodium malariae*
                                                          Plasmodium ovale
                                                          Plasmodium vivax

✦✦✦

Malaria is not a disease of the past as we dreamed in the 1950's. It has returned with the added complications of many strains which are resistant to the drugs used for treatment. The Malaria Foundation of Global Networks Against Malaria estimates (1997) that new cases occur at a rate of 300-500 million per year. An accurate count is not available because the majority of cases occur in developing countries which lack adequate medical and reporting facilities. Most of the several million that die are children under age five.

The following maps, redrawn from U.N. data, show the countries most affected and those at greatest risk. Sporadic cases occur in other countries; most of these are travelers from endemic and epidemic areas, although some are thought to originate locally even in the United States.

* *

☐ Areas in which malaria has disappeared or never existed.

▨ Areas with limited risk.

■ Areas where malaria transmission occurs.

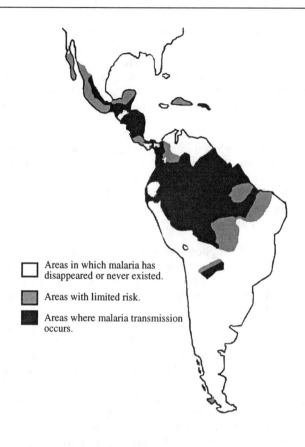

Areas in which malaria has disappeared or never existed.

Areas with limited risk.

Areas where malaria transmission occurs.

* *

Malaria is caused by four different species of parasites classified in the Genus *Plasmodium*. All are transmitted from infected persons to new victims by bites of several mosquitoes of the Genus *Anopheles*. *P. falciparum* produces the most severe form of malaria and most of the fatalities. *P. vivax* and *P. ovale* usually produce milder infections, but can remain inactive in the liver for several months and cause a relapse. *P. malariae* can remain dormant for many years, but is more susceptible to drug treatment than the others.

The threat of malaria was greatly reduced after World War II by massive spraying with DDT and other insecticides to reduce mosquito populations. When the dangerous side effects of DDT were discovered these efforts were curtailed and mosquito populations began to increase. In areas such as the southern United States all cases were treated and the reservoir of parasites was lost.

Drug resistance has developed in many strains of malaria parasites, further strengthening resurgence of the disease. For example, during the last five years there has been a seven-fold increase in deaths in Senegal, attributed to chloroquin resistance developing. Other African countries where most malaria cases occur, are beginning to experience the same problem.

Malaria researchers throughout the world are fearful of spread of the disease to temperate zone countries as a result of human travel and accidental transport of the vectors. Sporadic cases are already beginning to occur in the United States, which still has a good supply of *Anopheles* mosquitoes.

What is the answer? A basic approach is being attempted by the U.N. to start where the problem is worst--Africa. In late 1997, it will convene a multi-national multi-agency meeting to make plans for what will be called the African Malaria Initiative. The preliminary agenda calls for several different approaches to address the problems of malaria control and prevention. Information about the meeting will be published in the journal, **NATURE**, and publicized on its website (1997). The program to be proposed will begin in the year 2000 and require an estimated 30 years.

Dr. Deogratias Barakamfitye, Director of Malaria Control at the African center of WHO suggests that the first need is attitude adjustment. "Countries seem to accept that living with malaria is inevitable" he has said. Acceptance of dead children is a way of life that draws little attention from political leaders. The old economic law of guns or butter is working in some countries which spend over half their national budgets on arms.

Solving the scientific problems will probably be much easier than dealing with the social and economic ones.

Dr. Stephanie James, Chief of the Parasitology and International Programs Branch of NIAID, has stressed that understanding how different strains of malaria act is fundamental to other research. Doing so will lead into the new sciences of genetic epidemiology and molecular epidemiology. For example, Doumbo *et al* (1997) have reported evidence of infection by more than one strain of parasite in some patients in Mali.

Past attempts to produce an effective vaccine for malaria have been notoriously unsuccessful. New methods often bring new hope. Stoute *et al* (1997) have reported a new method of using recombinant peptides to produce a vaccine which is showing some promise in very small preliminary trials. It is called the RTS,S vaccine. The recombinant parasite protein is produced by yeast cells and fused with a hepatitis B surface protein.

Myocarditis--Another New One?

Myocarditis   Coxsackie Virus (?)
◆ ◆

On June 6, 1997, the World Health Organization issued an
Emerging and Communicable Disease Report about a possible
new disease outbreak in Sibu, Sarawak, Malaysia.

The Sarawak Health Department had reported 17 deaths due to
cardiogenic shock of unknown etiology in children age five months
to four years. The cases had all occurred since April 14. Symptoms
included fever, nervous system involvement, pulmonary edema,
seizures, and terminal cardiogenic shock due to myocarditis.
Laboratory testing of a variety of specimens ruled out a number
of causes, including dengue, yellow fever, rickettsia, and Japanese
encephalitis.

On the date of the report, other tests were still underway. Attending
physicians and health officials observed lesions on the palms and
lining of the mouth of some victims. These were a clue pointing
to the possibility of a Coxsackie virus such as that causing foot
and mouth disease in livestock.

By June 10, the number of deaths had increased to 21, and suspicion
of Coxsackie etiology became stronger. Laboratory results from
the Institute for Medical Research of Malaysia confirmed the
presence of antibodies to Coxsackie B virus in body fluids of
four of the victims. In the meantime, health departments were
receiving reports of a milder form of hand, foot, and mouth
disease in children from nearby areas. Some of them also had
Coxsackie B antibodies.

A week later on June 17, the number of deaths had increased to
26. Reports were being received of isolation of enterovirus from
specimens sent to CDC in the United States and Queen Mary
Hospital at the University of Hong Kong.

Since Coxsackie virus is transmitted primarily by fecal contamination, the Sarawak Health Department instituted a strong program of warning about the need for good personal hygiene coupled with increased efforts to control roach and fly populations. To decrease contact of children with each other, nurseries, kindergartens, and public swimming pools were closed. Close surveillance of family members of all cases has been instituted.

Have you ever read a mystery novel, and just as it approached the climax and you were about to find out "who done it" you discovered the last three pages of the book had been torn out? Such must be the case here as the presstime deadline approaches. Sorry about that! However, you can probably pursue the story at the Emerging and Communicable Disease website of WHO at http://www.who.ch/programmes/emc/news.htm.

Nosocomial Infections and Antibiotic Resistance

Nosocomial Infections   Many Organisms
Hospital Infections
◆ ◆

Think about the last time you experienced that awful sinking
feeling when you thought everything was going perfectly and
suddenly disaster emerged. You know the kind of thing--like
when you have just finished a great meal at a nice restaurant and
then realize you don't have your billfold. Will they call the
police, or just make you wash dishes the rest of the night?

Such an event is mild compared with the concern striking many
scientists as a result of increasing resistance of many bacteria to
the antibiotics used to combat their infections. In the strictest
sense, these are neither new bacteria nor new diseases. They are
changed bacteria which are producing newly uncontrollable
infections. The changes have resulted from mutations, adaptations,
or recombinations as described in Chapter 1.

In the early days of the antibiotic age only a few scientists voiced
concern when some organisms became resistant to penicillin or
the sulfas. After all, new antibiotics such as erythromycin, the
tetracyclines, and chloramphenicol were being discovered
regularly. They could handle the challenge. As time passed,
many pathogens developed multi-drug resistance. Even
Vancomycin, which worked well when other treatments failed, is
now becoming useless with many bacteria.

Many of the worst problems are what are called nosocomial
infections--those acquired by a patient or staff in a hospital or
other health care facility environment. When the potential
seriousness of the problem became apparent in the late 1950's,
many progressive hospitals established infection control
procedures. Since that time such practices have been expanded
to meet increasing needs. Unfortunately, the number of resistant
species multiplied and by 1990 had become a matter of worldwide
concern. The spread of Vancomycin resistant strains has prompted
CDC (1995) to adopt a formal program to control further increases.

The program does not operate from a central authority, but depends upon individual hospitals to apply the recommendations which include the following areas.

1. Each hospital should have an infection control program involving all departments.

2. Recognizing that misuse of antibiotics is a major factor in resistance development, the foundation of all programs should involve prudent vancomycin use. The report defines five situations in which the use of Vancomycin is appropriate or acceptable. Fourteen other common uses of vancomycin are situations in which it should be discouraged.

3. Continuing education programs should be established for all hospital personnel including physicians and medical students.

4. Laboratory facilities should be upgraded as needed to insure rapid identification of vancomycin resistant bacteria. This includes facilities which do not have a present problem.

5. Aggressive infection control procedures should be used to prevent spread of the nosocomial infections into the community by discharged patients or hospital personnel.

6. Patients with resistant infections should be treated in isolation with strict aseptic techniques, including appropriate disinfection of potential fomites such as doorknobs, bed rails, etc.

7. Establish procedures for prompt reporting of all resistant infections.

The recommendations listed above have much merit; however, they may require modification in the light of newly developing knowledge. Dr. Keiichi Hiramatsu of Juntendo University in Tokyo has expressed concern (1997) about low levels of resistance in *Staphylococcus aureus* and has developed a procedure for detecting such organisms when they would be missed by current standard procedures. His work is important because, historically, resistance has progressed from low to high levels over time.

The range of resistance is widespread and involves many serious diseases. It also may be a factor in problems resulting from species which in the past have been considered normal flora of the body and non-pathogenic such as *Staphylococcus epidermidis*. Other organisms such as the enterococci which are normal inhabitants of the digestive and female genital tracts have been known to cause infections in other organs, but these were always considered to result from the patient's own bacteria. Now, there is increasing evidence of person-to person transmission of resistant strains.

O'nyong-Nyong Fever

O'nyong-Nyong Fever   **O'nyong-Nyong Virus**
♦ ♦

The emergence of O'nyong-nyong fever in Africa has occurred in epidemic form after an absence of 35 years. Just before our deadline for completion of this book, E. B. Rwaguma *et al* (1997) reported increasing incidence of the disease which was first noted in Uganda in late 1996. By March, 1997, it had spread into neighboring districts of Uganda and crossed the international border into Tanzania. Dr. Rwaguma noted that the last previous occurrence of the disease was in an epidemic which lasted two years in Uganda, Kenya, Tanzania, and Zambia. Since that epidemic ended in 1961, no cases have been reported until the present outbreak began.

The disease is thought to have a viral etiology, presently referred to as the O'nyong-nyong virus. Transmission is hypothesized to be by mosquitoes. Research is now being conducted at the Center for Disease Control and Prevention to prove the validity of this theory. The threat of worldwide spread of mosquito species formerly found in only isolated geographic areas is cause for concern that the disease might also spread.

Little is known about the virus since we did not have the tools of modern biotechnology in 1961. DNA studies are in progress and preliminary immunologic research indicates that victims probably develop serum antibodies to the viral antigen. Virus has been isolated from suspected cases by injecting the patient's serum samples into baby mice. The virus is apparently able to multiply in the mice. The fact that the virus can cross species lines immediately raises the possibility that the disease might have a natural host reservoir in lower animals. That remains to be seen.

O'nyong-nyong fever is not considered a fatal disease, although it is severely debilitating. No deaths have occurred to date in the present epidemic; miscarriages have occurred in infected pregnant females. The morbidity rate in areas affected by the epidemic is high with 60 to 80 per cent of the population becoming infected. There appear to be no age or sex differences in susceptibility.

Since at present there is no treatment except supportive, it is fortunate that the disease is self-limiting. That is not synonymous with mild. Symptoms are severe. The name of the disease provides a clue to its nature. In the Acholi dialect of Uganda, "O'nyong nyong" means a weakening of the joints. Initially there is high fever with skin rash followed quickly by severe arthritis, particularly in the larger joints. This is soon accompanied by swollen lymph nodes, chest pain and severe pain in the eyes. Technical descriptions of the symptoms include general malaise, which is probably the unnecessary understatement of all time. Who wouldn't feel "blah" with all that other?

This one bears watching. Today, Africa is no longer the dark continent, totally isolated from the rest of the world.

Pfiesteriosis

Pfiesteri infections   *Pfiesteria piscicida*
Pfiesteria poisoning
◆◆

No one is sure about this one yet, but in late 1997 it appears we may have something new to worry about. Pfiesteriosis is an infection of fish caused by a dinoflagellate known as *Pfiesteria piscidia*. The characteristics of the organism were described by Burkholder *et al* (1992). The dinoflagellates are a group of marine microorganisms best known for producing red tides. Most species release compounds which are toxic to marine life.

During the summer of 1997, *P. piscidia* attracted great attention as a result of blooms and consequent fish kills in the Chesapeake Bay and other regions of Southeastern U.S. coastal areas. A major problem in studying the organism and the infections it causes is that it exists in several different forms (Steidenger *et al*, 1996).

By late summer and early fall, 1997, numerous human infection reports, most unconfirmed and in the popular press, began to appear. Later reports hinted that exposure to the toxins might cause some short term memory loss as well as skin injury.

Studies are underway to learn more about the human infections, fish kills, and effects of fertilizer runoffs into bays and estuaries. Unfortunately, at the time of this review, more questions than answers have been raised.

Public fears, often fed by inaccurate news reports prompted the University of Maryland, in cooperation with other government and health agencies, to establish a *Pfiesteria* web site to provide trustworthy information. New developments will be reported there as research continues.

Prostatitis

Prostatitis   Unknown
Prostatitic hypertrophy
◆ ◆

We've had the disease, often unrecognized in its true form with
cause unknown. Is the etiologic agent about to emerge, or perhaps
more accurately, be dragged out?

The prostate gland, a male accessory sex organ located deep in
the pelvic cavity, has historically been the major site of problems
in the male reproductive system. The problems usually fit into at
least one of three categories:

1. Prostatitis - infection of the gland

2. Benign prostatic hypertrophy - enlargement of the prostate
   which is usually associated with benign hyperplasia, an
   excessive multiplication of cells of the organ.

3. Prostate cancer.

Prostatitis can occur at any age and is frequently seen in young
men. It has been estimated that at least 50 per cent of all males
will suffer from prostatitis sometime during their lives.
Hypertrophy is a slow gradual process, usually first becoming
apparent in middle age or later. The typical prostate cancer does
not occur until late middle or old age.

Hennefent (1997) has recently raised some thought-provoking
questions about the true incidence of prostatitis and the possibility
that it is caused by an unrecognized bacterium. Many bacteria
are not culturable by traditional methods and consequently would
not be associated with a disease if such methods were the only
tests used. He suggests that new molecular approaches such as
those described by Gao and Moore (1996) be used.

The importance of early correct diagnosis and treatment of prostatitis is obvious when one considers the possibility of a relationship between prostatitis and prostate cancer. For example, McNeal (1995) found that prostatitis lesions were present in approximately half the men who underwent biopsies for possible prostate cancer. The relation between prostatitis and benign hypertrophy may be even stronger. An early study (Bostrom, 1971) of 100 men autopsied following death by unrelated causes such as accidents, showed the presence of prostatitis in 22 per cent of men under age 40; it was present in 60 per cent of older men. Later, Kohnen (1979) found evidence of prostatitis in 98 per cent of men suffering from hypertrophy.

Hennenfent (1997) points out that since prostatitis is a major infectious disease of presently unknown cause, it needs more application of the new technologies, including the possibility of DNA vaccines.

Salmonellosis

Only a few years after Robert Koch proved that bacteria cause disease, a U. S. veterinarian, Dr. Daniel E. Salmon, isolated and described a previously unknown enteric organism. Within a short time many related varieties were found and they were classified in the new genus, *Salmonella,* named in honor of Salmon. With continuing discoveries of new varieties, the genus has become huge, now numbering over 2200 strains. Most are pathogenic, causing diseases ranging from mild gastroenteritis to fatal systemic infections.

Since 1980, the number of human infections has increased dramatically. According to a WHO Fact Sheet (#139, 1997), several European countries have experienced a 20-fold increase during the last ten years. Equally disturbing is the emergence of many new antibiotic resistant varieties since 1990.

The genus *Salmonella* is divided into three groups on the basis of their human and lower animal hosts.

Group 1 includes some of the most severe pathogens such as *S. typhi* and *S. paratyphi* which cause severe, often fatal infections in only humans and other higher primates.

Group 2 includes pathogens which ordinarily infect only certain animals such as *S. choleraesuis* in pigs. Many of these strains are capable of crossing over to humans and causing life threatening infections.

Group 3 is the catch-all for the rest. Most cause relatively mild gastroenteritis, but can produce dangerous infections particularly in the very young, elderly, and immunocompromised. Major organisms in this group include *S. enteriditis* and *S. typhimurium*, both of which are transmitted to man from lower animals.

Most cases of salmonellosis are acquired individually from undercooked food sources. This does not mean that widespread outbreaks cannot occur when thousands of people consume food from the same contaminated source. Sometimes particular types of foods are associated with specific organisms such as the relationship of *S. typhimurium* with poultry and egg products. In contrast, *S. enteriditis* is associated with a wide variety of meat, meat products, milk, eggs, and poultry.

Direct human to human transmission is unusual. Most human involvement is related to fecal contamination of foods by infected or carrier handlers.

Multi-drug resistance seems to be rapidly becoming a major concern. The situation in England and Wales which have comparatively good reporting systems, is an example of the problem. Multi-drug resistance was associated with only approximately 300 cases in 1990; by 1996, the number had increased to around 3,500. Also during that six years, the number of antibiotics becoming ineffective also increased.

The WHO report cited above notes that no country in the world has the knowledge and technology to provide pathogen-free fresh meat and poultry products. It provides a somewhat pessimistic outlook for limiting the increase of salmonellosis.

Sadly, the wonders of modern biotechnology become less impressive when the primary recommendation for controlling a major increasing disease incidence is to emphasize the need for cooking food thoroughly before consumption.

Tuberculosis

TB   *Mycobacterium tuberculosis*
Consumption
Galloping consumption
◆ ◆

One of every seven deaths in Europe and the Americas was ascribed to tuberculosis in 1882, when Robert Koch announced identification of the etiologic agent. The CDC in 1997 estimated that over 200 million people have died of TB since Koch's discovery. WHO estimates about eight million new cases per year with about three million deaths throughout the world.

The first antibiotics effective against *M. tuberculosis* became available in the early 1950's and the disease was virtually wiped out in the United States by 1960. Unfortunately, such was not the case in much of the rest of the world because of limited medical facilities. Suddenly, in 1985 in the U.S., the downward incidence of new cases reversed and there was a sharp increase during the next seven years. Fig 2.5 shows the reported cases from 1975 to 1995.

* *

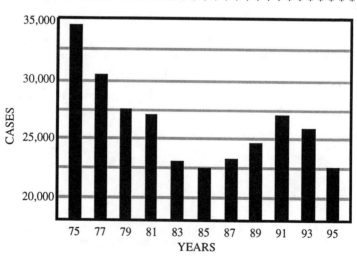

Fig. 2.5. Reported cases of TB from 1975-1995.

The CDC attributes the increased number of cases to three major factors:

1. Immigration from other countries. Cases in foreign-born accounted for 60% of the new infectious.

2. HIV. Immunocompromised persons are much more susceptible.

3. Increased transmission in closed populations such as prisons, hospitals, homeless shelters, etc.

Related and contributing to all the problems was the fact that many of the organizations involved with TB control and prevention had ceased to exist after the decline in cases through the 1960's and '70's.

To stem the tide of increasing incidence in the U.S., in 1992, the National Institute of Allergy and Infectious Disease (NIAID) developed a new research program which required an eight-fold increase in funding over 1991. The goals of the program are shown in Table 2.1.

Table 2.1
NIAID TB Research Agenda

- Studies of the epidemiology and natural history of TB.

- Basic research into the biology of TB.

- Development of new tools to diagnose TB.

- Development of new TB drugs or new ways to deliver standard drugs.

- Clinical trials of anti-TB therapies.

- Development of new vaccines to prevent TB.

- Training to increase the number of TB researchers.

* *

Drug treatment is a major problem with TB. A major concern of health officials in late 1997 has become the development of *M. tuberculosis* strains which are resistant to one or more of the formerly effective medications. Resistance occurs in this organism by the same mechanisms previously described for others.

A complicating factor is present in TB therapy. To be effective, the drugs must be taken over a period of 6-12 months. The NIAID estimates that in some U.S. cities about half the persons being treated do not take the drugs for the prescribed period of time. Such short term or low level exposure gives the bacteria a better chance to adapt and become resistant.

Carelessness and complacency also play a part, especially in nosocomial tuberculosis. Agerton *et al* (1997) described transmission of a drug-resistant strain of TB to eight patients by improperly sterilized bronchoscopes in a New York hospital. Michele *et al* (1997) applied DNA fingerprinting to suspected bronchoscopic transmission. The pattern of the organism from the second patient was identical to that of the first. This technique leaves little room for doubt.

The incidents just described were sufficiently alarming to provoke some unusually pointed editorial comment in the Journal of the American Medical Association (Wenzel and Edmond, 1997). They emphasized the need for strict adherence to sterilization protocols and infection control practices.

Again, the weak link in the chain.

With the tuberculosis rate increase already above that earlier predicted for the year 2000, the reader might wish to keep up with new developments. Both NIAID and CDC have excellent web sites to provide reliable information with emphasis on U.S. conditions. WHO sites provide international data.

Venezuelan Equine Encephalitis

Venezuelan Equine Encephalitis   VEE Virus
VEE Disease
◆ ◆

The virus which causes Venezuelan equine encephalitis is quite distinct from those involved in the more common eastern and western equine encephalitis well known in the United States.

The Venezuelan virus was actually first reported in Columbia in 1935. Presumably the name results from the fact that the first severe outbreak of the disease occurred as an epizootic in Venezuela in 1938. From there it seems to have spread to Equador, Trinidad, and Panama during the ensuing five years. There is now a distinct threat of spread throughout South America and even possibly into North America with the number of cases suddenly starting to increase. Animal hosts for the virus do not appear to be limited to horses. Many lower animals are apparently capable of harboring the virus and are able to transmit it through insect vectors. The primary mosquito vector is probably *Aedes taeniorhynchus* which is capable of transmitting the virus between horses and humans.

An unusual feature of transmission of disease of this type is the fact that the VEE virus can also apparently be transmitted through the upper respiratory track as a droplet, or as a dust borne infection.

The clinical picture of the disease is relatively mild when compared with other forms of encephalitis. The incubation period ranges from two to five days following exposure. The symptoms are actually more cold or influenza like than what would typically be expected in a neurologic infection. There is fever, lethargy, gastrointestinal discomfort, and upper respiratory symptoms. The death rate is quite low which is fortunate, since as with other viral disease, there is not at present a good treatment. During the decade following first discovery of the disease, only two human deaths were reported.

In view of the relatively mild nature of VEE, a major public health concern is that of possible mutation of the virus which might result in either a higher level of virulence or expansion of its host and vector range.

Vibrio vulnificus - An "Impossible" Infection

Vulnificus diarrhea   *Vibrio vulnificus*
Vulnificus septicemia
◆ ◆

Marine microorganisms have traditionally been of little public
health concern because it was popularly believed that such
halophilic (salt-loving) species could not survive in a low salt
environment, including that of the human body. That theory
now rests in peace along with the idea that the earth is flat. We
have become aware of *Vibrio vulnificus*, a relative of the species
that causes cholera.

This organism lives in warm seawater, often contaminating
seafood, especially oysters. Consumption of such improperly
cooked seafood results in severe diarrhea, vomiting, and abdominal
pain. The infection can spread from the digestive system into the
blood, causing a septicemia which has a mortality rate of around
50 per cent.

Ingestion is not the only source of problems. The organism can
cause severe skin infections when open wounds are exposed to
seawater.

Since infections caused by *V. vulnificus* infections are not a
reportable disease, the extent of their occurrence is unknown.
Another problem is missed diagnosis. Standard bacteriology
procedures performed in medical laboratories will not detect the
organism because of its high salt requirement. Despite all this,
CDC recorded over 300 cases between 1988 and 1995. Most of
these occurred in the Gulf Coast states.

Most seafood transmitted diseases are associated with fecal
contamination of the food. Such is not the case with *V. vulnificus*
infections since the organism is present in uncontaminated legal
harvest waters.

Control of the disease is based on frequent monitoring of coastal waters for the organism. Prevention is largely a matter of individual responsibility. Seafood, especially shellfish, should be thoroughly cooked and persons with skin lesions should avoid entering warm salty or brackish water.

Yellow Fever

Yellow Fever   Yellow Fever Virus
◆ ◆

The early medical history of yellow fever is unclear. There is
debate about whether the origin of the disease was in Africa or
Central and South America. The first documented cases that
meet modern descriptions were found in the Yucatan in 1648.
During the next three centuries the disease was found to be
widespread throughout South and Central America. It was recorded
in North America along the East Coast and in the Gulf Coast
states. Presumably, the disease spread from South and Central
America to southern US ports and was then carried northward.

Yellow fever was a major problem for the military in the Spanish
American War in 1898. Likewise, it almost prevented completion
of the Panama Canal. Much of our modern knowledge of Yellow
Fever is based on the work of the Yellow Fever Commission
which was appointed to deal with the problem. Major Walter
Reed, who was in charge of the commission in Cuba and other
areas of Central America, carried out studies which led to
understanding the processes of transmission and provided a basis
for eradication of the disease by controlling mosquitoes.

The primary vector of the Yellow Fever Virus is *Aedes aegypti.*
The most common means of transmission is man - mosquito -
man; other possible sources exist. Many monkeys, some rodents,
and other animals are capable of harboring the Yellow Fever
Virus. Mosquitoes other than *A. aegypti* may also serve as vectors.
Occasional cases occur as a direct contamination of the skin by
virus containing fluids.

The present reemergence of Yellow Fever is directly related to
increasing mosquito populations resulting from urbanization and
changes in breeding waters.

During an epidemic, the incubation period from mosquito borne virus infection is five to six days. There is a sudden onset of fever which reaches a maximum of around 103 °F on the first or second day. The fever is accompanied by severe headache and backache. Most patients experience nausea and vomiting. The face becomes swollen and congested and bleeding may occur from the gums. Vomitus is typically the type referred to as coffee grounds with a dark brownish-black appearance resulting from gastric hemorrhage. There is usually a marked drop in blood pressure and jaundice appears as a result of liver congestion. Severe destruction of kidney tissues may occur, resulting in abnormal nitrogen waste excretion.

The overall death rate from Yellow Fever infections is difficult to assess because the disease apparently also occurs in a subclinical form which is not diagnosed. Likewise, there is disagreement as to the severity of the disease in children compared with adults.

The research done by Reed *et al* (1911) demonstrated that the virus is available to the mosquito during the first three days of clinical disease. They also showed that the virus remains in the mosquito for about twelve days before transmission to another person.

The biology of host-parasite relationships received much attention during the 1920's and 1930's. Finally, by 1937 it was established that the virus actually multiplies in the body of the mosquito but does no harm to that host.

As with any other mosquito borne disease, control of the vector will be the greatest problem faced by the World Health Organization as it seeks to contain the current increase in the number of Yellow Fever cases.

New Disease of Non-Human Life

Our story of new and emerging diseases would be incomplete without recognition of new infections in plants and lower animals. While discussion of specific problems is beyond the scope of this review, these new and reemerging diseases are of vital importance because they affect our food supply and in some cases may spread directly to humans. A horrifying example is given in the Epilogue.

Many of the lower animal diseases are developing in the same way as their human counterparts. Natural evolutionary changes in the pathogenic microorganisms result in new hosts or increased virulence. Ecological factors such as overcrowding and habitat loss contribute to new outbreaks.

Some of the "new" plant diseases are really old ones wreaking havoc on new varieties of plant hosts. Intensive artificial selective breeding of plants to obtain one or two desirable traits often results in loss of natural genetic defenses of the original cultivates. As with humans and lower animals, natural evolutionary processes including genetic recombinations in the pathogens result in new diseases.

Like it or not, when we get down to basic biological processes, there is little difference between humans, lower animals, and plants. Only a very few DNA sequences distinguish us.

Readers who would like to follow the progress of these new diseases can find a reliable unlimited resource at ProMED.

Section III

Control & Prevention

Section III

Control & Prevention

Will the new and emerging diseases wipe out the world as we know it? Will the survivors be the bacteria, viruses, and the protein soups of viroids and prions left to restart the long evolutionary process? It could happen--much sooner and much easier than most people think. Being unaware of the horrifying potential or ignoring it will not make it go away. Are the warning voices of a few public health authorities being heard? Apparently not well. In the western industrialized civilizations, we feel secure in our complacent attitude of "It can't happen here."

But, it is already starting to happen here. Prevention and control procedures are being designed. It is time to listen.

The Program For Prevention and Control

History clearly reflects the difficulties of getting every country in the world to agree on anything. A remarkable exception is the effort to prevent and control the emerging infections. Essentially identical goals and recommendations from almost every nation as well as the UN underscore the dangers we face. The recommendations of world health authorities can be summarized as four major points:

- Surveillance and response
- Applied research
- Prevention and control
- Public health infrastructure

These are broad-based approaches applicable to all diseases. They are supplemented by special localized procedures for specific diseases such as nosocomial infections.

Let's examine what these international proposals mean and consider their implications for our survival. Then, we shall examine some of the problems which must be overcome.

Surveillance is the cornerstone of the whole program. In order to respond appropriately to a disease outbreak, public health authorities must be aware of it immediately. This means constant monitoring and prompt reporting by the local medical establishment throughout the world. With modern rapid transportation to spread a disease, a few hours can make a critical difference. Authority for response must be in place before the outbreak. There will not be time for legislative bodies to argue.

Applied research means making discoveries of new diagnostic techniques available to epidemiologists. The availability must be a practical one with techniques that can be used anywhere, not just where laboratory facilities are available. A second aspect of applied research is the development of new methods to control an outbreak.

Prevention and control strategies are dependent upon the awareness of the problem. More effective communication of the problems to both the public and medical personnel is a primary goal. A CDC report (1994) stresses the need to make physicians in training and in practice aware of the needs and problems. Another aspect of these strategies involves the integration of behavioral science into the epidemiologic and medical approaches.

The fourth goal of the programs for prevention and control is simply designated "Infrastructure." This translates into strengthening local and national public health organizations ranging from laboratories to data analysis.

Dr. David Satcher of the CDC has reviewed (1995) the history of infectious disease control and prevention and related it to present efforts. Reflecting on the historical perspective, he describes our present situation as "...a fragile equilibrium between humans and infectious microorganisms."

The extent of the fragility described by Satcher is made frighteningly clear when we consider some of the problems in implementing the recommended goals.

Surveillance and Quick Response

No matter how sophisticated and complete control programs are, they do no good if those responsible for implementing them are unaware of a problem. Continuous surveillance is the basis of awareness. Let's use the present system in the United States as the horrible example, although there are worse, and in many parts of the world there are none.

Berkelman *et al* (1994) described infectious disease surveillance in the United States as "A Crumbling Foundation." They reviewed a number of policy problems and gave a number of really scary examples of outbreaks which were not properly controlled. Many of the problems noted by these researchers seem to originate in the surveillance and reporting procedures used.

In the United States, prevention and control relies mainly on a notifiable disease system which theoretically should work, but in reality often does not. Figure 3.1 on the next page shows the pattern surveillance and reporting should follow.

Even when the reporting system works, response in the U.S. may be severely limited because there is no executive function for response. According to a federal report (CISET, 1996), several other factors may prevent timely response, especially when the disease threat originates in other countries.

Although CDC has the expertise, it lacks authority to intervene in outbreaks outside the United States. About all it can do is quarantine obviously ill travelers at ports of entry and issue travelers warnings with respect to countries which have epidemics.

Other agencies such as the Federal Emergency Management Administration and USAID's Office of Foreign Disaster Assistance do not have legal authority to recognize infectious diseases as emergencies. The U.S. Department of Agriculture is charged with preventing the importation of food-borne and animal-borne diseases. Obviously the system does not work well; if it did, we would not have descriptions of such outbreaks in Section II.

Another weakness is funding. Almost two-thirds of the CDC budget is earmarked for control and prevention of infectious diseases. That sounds good until one examines the details. About 95 per cent of that budget item is designated for AIDS, tuberculosis, SID's, and vaccine preventable diseases.

The list of things you don't really want to know gets longer.

* *

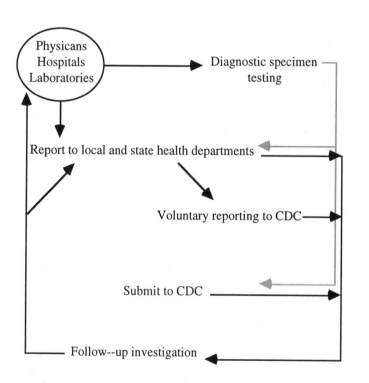

Fig. 3.1. Surveillance and Reporting

Communication

Some of the most serious problems in containment of new and emerging infections are not of a medical or other scientific basis. They are problems of rapid worldwide communication.

Prevention or control of an epidemic outbreak must be done quickly; the consequences of even a few days delay could easily be millions of additional cases. The old protective barriers of national boundaries and distance no longer exist. World travel and trade provide means for rapid dissemination of the etiological agent. When a new disease appears today in Australia or Africa, the chances are good that it could be in North America next week. We need to know; likewise the Australians and Africans need to be aware of new outbreaks in the western hemisphere.

Under these conditions, the traditional methods of scientific research communication no longer work. One factor is time. Many months pass between the time a scientist submits his report to a journal and the time it appears in print. A related problem is the decreasing availability of periodicals to the scientific community. A few major publishers have a stranglehold on the peer reviewed periodicals and have increased subscription prices to the point that many laboratories and libraries are severely curtailing their holdings.

What about textbooks and monographs? Forget it -- publication and distribution of a new textbook takes about two years. Only the small independent publishers can do it faster, but they do not publish that type of material. Presentation of data at scientific meetings and conferences is faster, but may still require a year.

Electronic communication such as the weekly internet reports by the World Health Organization and Communicable Disease Center are a promising approach. Even these have their limitations. In reviewing the problems, Berger (1997) pointed out that such communication is hardly practical in parts of the world that lack adequate electrical and telephone service.

Another aspect of slow scientific communication is the peer review process. We dare not try to do without it. Anyone who thinks this safety cloak is not needed should look critically at all the pseudoscience garbage on the WWW. Perhaps a partial answer lies in a second internet to fulfill the need for rapid scientific communication; after all, that was the original purpose. Even this, however, would not solve the problems discussed by Berger.

Human Behavior

The ultimate barrier to effective prevention and control was described earlier as the weak link in the chain - human behavior. The obvious example is found in the increasing morbidity of STD's such as AIDS, genital herpes. and chlamydia infections. The numbers of cases have become staggering despite all the warnings and education efforts directed to avoiding unprotected sexual activity. The most unbelievable part of this is the objections many parents still have to providing such education for their children.

The New Technologies

Applications of new technology are not limited to communication and computerized databases. Several new biological technologies are being investigated.

One of the most fascinating is transgenic mosquitoes. Scientists have long known that many strains of mosquitoes, including some *Anopheles gambia*, are naturally resistant to infestation by malaria parasites. An international cooperative effort to map the genes of resistant mosquitoes has been started. Frank Collins (Collins *et al*, 1996) at CDC has been working on the project with Fetis Kafates (Kafates *et al*, 1997) of the European Molecular Biology laboratory in Heidelberg. They have found several genes that are involved in natural resistance.

Another approach is that of Julian Crampton and his colleagues at the Liverpool School of Tropical Medicine in England. They have found a mammalian gene for an antibody which attacks one stage of the malaria parasite (Crampton *et al*, 1996). Their next step is to insert the gene into mosquito vectors.

Malaria is not the only disease for which the use of transgenic mosquitoes is of interest. Olson et al (1996) at Colorado State University are investigating a gene which blocks reproduction of the Dengue Fever virus in mosquitoes.

Mobile portions of foreign genes like those described are called transposons. The idea is to insert them into mosquitoes which will then be released into the wild population where they will replicate and become part of the population's genome. We do not yet know if this will work with mosquitoes; it does work quite well with fruitflies in laboratory studies.

As is the case with any genetically engineered organism released into a wild population, there are potential inherent dangers which should be addressed before the experiments are done. These will need to be balanced against the problems of other methods of insect control. Vector biologists are acknowledging that traditional chemical attempts to eliminate insect populations are doomed to failure.

Epilogue

Reviewing the scientific literature leads to the inevitable question of whether or not the microbial attacks can be prevented or controlled. Neither human history nor biologic principles provide encouragement. Whenever a population has become overcrowded and one species has encroached upon another, disaster has resulted.

The literature points to a complex involving politics, media hype, and public awareness as well as the medical professions and epidemiology.

Residents of industrialized nations have little concept of disease problems in less developed parts of the world. The difficulties facing epidemiologists are profoundly illustrated by the following description of a possible new hemorrhagic fever in Kenya. (ProMED mail moderator Martin Hugh-Jones, DVM, personal communication, Jan. 2, 1998.)

* *

[The following report is thanks to Dr. Louise Martin, DVM, and Dr. Doug Klaucke, MD, Acting WHO Representative in Nairobi, who corrected and updated (Thu, 01 Jan 1998 13:06:02 +0300) my original draft of Dr. Martin's Monday conversation with me. You cannot get closer to the horse's mouth than this and we at ProMED-mail greatly appreciate their sharing this information. We look forward to updates. Dr. Martin is presently on her way back to Garissa. - Mod.MHJ]

On Monday (12-29-97), I spoke by telephone with my ex student Dr. Louise Martin, who is in Garissa. She is the only veterinarian with the international team there and the only vet in the region known to be working on this outbreak.

On the animal side, thousands of livestock - cattle but especially sheep and goats - are dying or dead. Martin estimates the livestock mortality rate to be 50% to 75% in the area. The animals show a fever, with or without constipation, passing to diarrhea and snotty noses with or without blood, and then a terminal diarrhea (also with or without blood). There is a "viral soup" of conditions there, with a wide variety of conditions, some very suggestive of FMD (foot lesions but as yet she has seen no mouth lesions), foot rot, pleuropneumonia, you-name-it. The area has been without veterinary coverage for some time apparently due to severe flooding. Many of the dying and dead stock are being butchered and eaten. She has examined a 14 year-old girl who had just been taught how to butcher goats and who had fluid and pus-filled vesicular lesions on her hands, and lymphadenitis of axillary nodes. A frequently volunteered comment by the meat consumers is that the cooked meat is tasteless and soft like "over-ripe fruit", this is characteristic of high lactic acid levels. [Historically, this affected area is close to one of the areas where Rinderpest was not eradicated in the previous African campaign of the '60s & '70s. MHJ]

They have confirmed over 300 human deaths to date. Most died within 3-4 days, some within 12 hours, of falling ill. The condition characteristically starts with a high fever, bad headache, abdominal pain, passing to vomiting and diarrhea. If they vomit blood it is a lethal prognosis, passing to epistaxis, shock, and death. Because this area is affected by undernutrition, unclean drinking water, multiple diseases and limited health services it is difficult to estimate the number of non-fatal cases that may be occurring so an accurate estimate of the case fatality rate is not possible. So far they have only got to some 12-15 villages, but there has been a stream of people sent from further villages in attempts to get help. One very ill small boy who had been vomiting blood was treated with penicillin and is now sitting up in bed. The medical facilities there are less than minimal, compounded by the two months nurses strike. Treatment seems to be limited at this time to chloroquine and penicillin.

While the national government initially claimed that the "bleeding disease" is due to malaria (and there are plenty of mosquitoes and malaria), of the 22 samples checked in Nairobi for clinical malaria, none were positive. But this disease along with many others will be present in this area where there is extensive and widespread malnutrition. There is cholera in the same general area. Initial results of testing the [21] human serum samples at the National Institute of Virology in South Africa found no evidence of Ebola, Marburg, Chikungunya, Sindbis, West Nile Fever, dengue, tick-borne encephalitis complex, Lassa fever, Crimean Congo hemorrhagic fever, and hantaviruses. Sera tested at the Kenya Medical Research Institute in Nairobi were negative for yellow fever. Testing for anthrax and Rift Valley fever are not yet complete. There were three sera positive for IgG to _B. anthracis_ and one possibly positive for [PA] antigen. Four of 22 sera were positive by PCR for Rift Valley fever virus (RVFV) RNA. Three of these four were negative for IgM antibodies to RVFV antigens, so confirmatory tests are being done.

On the Somali side of the border the disease situation is very similar. Case finding there has been made harder by the Muslim need to bury corpses expeditiously.

The single telephone line is in to the International Red Cross compound. The health team of some 8 individuals is made up of the Provincial medical health staff, WHO, AMREF, Medicines sans Frontieres, International Red Cross, and Medicines du Monde. The Kenya army fled. Local transport to check villages is through the Rural Food Program vehicles. The tracks are soft, deep mud. Thanks to the rains some villages when reached are found to have been abandoned. There is one helicopter, and banditry. Thanks to the national election (29-30 December) and the holiday season (25 December through 30 December were all national holidays), it has been difficult to mobilize national government support. All ministers were running for re election and the country is between governments.

The investigation is expected to continue to confirm the diagnosis [or diagnoses], to obtain a better estimate of the magnitude of the problem, and to determine whether it is spreading. Prevention and treatment measures are also being planned.

* *

Frightening?

Yes, sometimes a cold clinical scientific description is more mesmerizing than overdramatized news presentations.

We can no longer hide behind our high technology in isolation from the extreme poverty and need in other countries. Our planet has become too small. If we attempt to become enshrouded by our geography or excuse our mental indolence by saying, "I don't understand science," we invite an early visit by the Angel of Death.

References

Agerton, Tracy, S. Valway, B. Gore, *et al* 1997. Transmission of a highly drug-resistant strain (Strain W-1) of *Mycobacterium tuberculosis*. *JAMA* **278**:1073-1077.

Altekruse, S.F., M.L. Cohen, and D.L. Swerdlow. 1997. Emerging food borne diseases. *Emerg. Inf. Dis.* **3**: No. 3.

Bendall, R.P., S. Lucas, A. Moody, G. Tovey, and P.L. Chiodini. 1993. Diarrhea associated with cyanobacterium-like bodies: a new coccidian enteritis of man. *Lancet* **341**: 590-592.

Berkelman, R.L., Bryan, R.T., Osterholm, M.T., LeDuc, J.W., Hughes, J.M. 1994. Infectious disease surveillance: a crumbling Foundation. *Science* **264** 368-70.

Besser, R.E., S.M. Lett, T. Weber, *et al.* 1993. An outbreak of diarrhea and hemolytic uremic syndrome from *Escherchia coli* 0157:H7 in fresh-pressed apple cider. *JAMA.* **269:** 2217-2220.

Bhattacharya, M.K., S.K. Bhattacharya, S. Garg, P.K. Saha, D. Dutta, G. Balakrish-Nair, B. Deb, and K. Das. 1993. Outbreak of *Vibrio cholerae* non-01 in India and Bangladesh. *Lancet* **341**: 1952-1956.

Boschert, K. 1994. Prions and transgenic animals New Zealand Veterinary J.

Boyce, T.G., D.L. Swerdlow, and P.M. Griffin. 1995. *Escherchia coli* 0157:H7 and the hemolyte-uremic syndrome. *N. Eng. J. Med.* **333:** 364-368.

Burkholder, J.M., E.J. Noga, C.W. Hobbs, H.B. Glasgow, Jr., and S.A. Smith 1992. New "phantom" dinoflagellate is the causeative agent of major estuarine fish kills. *Nature* **358**:407-410.

Carter, Craig, N., N.C. Ronald, J.H. Steele, *et al.* 1997. Knowledge-based screening for rare and emerging infections/parasitic disease: A case study of brucellosis and murine typhus. *Emerg. Inf. Dis.* **1:** No 1.

Centers for Disease Control and Prevention. 1994. Addressing emerging infectious disease threats: a prevention strategy for the United States. Atlanta, Georgia: US Dept. of Health and Human Services, Public Health Service,

Centers for Disease Control. 1990. Water borne disease outbreaks, 1986-1988. *MMWR CDC Surveill Summ* **39**: 1-13.

Chomel, B.B., R. Kasten, K. Floyd-Hawkins, B. Chi, K. Yamamoto, J. Roberts, A. Gurfield, R. Abbott, N. Pedersen, and J. Koehler. 1996. Experimental transmission of *Bartonella henselae* by the cat flea. *J. Clin. Microbiol.* **34**: 1952-1956.

Cohen, M.L. 1992. Epidemiology of drug resistance: implications for a post-antimicrobial era. *Science* **257**:1050-5.

Colwell, R.R. 1996. Global climate and infectious disease: The Cholera Paradigm. *Science* **274**: 2025-2031.

Cordell, R.L., Addiss, D.G. 1994. Cryptosporidiosis in child care settings: a review of the literature and recommendations for prevention and control. *Pediatr. Infect. Dis. J.* **13**: 311-317.

Davies, J. 1994. Inactivation of antibiotics and the dissemination of resistance genes. *Science* **264**: 375-82.

Dhondt, A.A. 1996. Finch disease update. *Birdscope* **10**: 4.

Dolan, M.J., Wong, M.T., Regnery, R.L. *et al.* 1993. Syndrome of *Rochalimaea henselae* adenitis suggesting cat scratch disease, *Ann Intern Med* **118**: 331-6.

Dubos, René, J. 1952. Bacterial and Mycotic Infections of Man. 2nd ed. J.B. Lippincott Company, Philadelphia.

Edwards, J.F. and K. Hendricks, 1997. Lack of serological evidence for an association between Cache Valley virus infection and amencephaly and other neural tube defects in Texas. *Emerg. Inf. Dis.* **3:** No 1.

Epstein, P.R., Ford, T.E., Colwell, R.R. 1993. Marine ecosystems, *Lancet* **342**:1216-9.

Epstein, P.R., Rogers, D.J., Slooff, R. 1993. Satellite imaging and vector-borne disease. *Lancet* **341**:1404-6.

Epstein, P.R., Ford, T.E., Colwell, R.R. 1993. Marine ecosystems, *Lancet* **342**:1216-9.

First International Conference on Emerging Zoonoses. 1996. (see Meslin, F.-X., 1997).

Galanti, G. A. 1991. Caring For Patients From Different Cultures. University of Pennsylvania Press, Philadelphia.

Goldstein, S.T., D.D. Juranek, O. Ravenholt, *et al.* 1996. Cryptospoidiosis:: An outbreak associated with drinking water despite state-of-the-art water treatment. *Ann. Inf. Med.* **124:** 459.

Groce, N. E. and M. E. Reeve, 1996. Traditional healers and global surveillance strategies for emerging diseases: Closing the gap. *Emerg. Inf. Dis.* **2**: No. 4.

Gubler, D.J., Trent, D.W. 1993. Emergence of epidemic dengue/dengue hemorrhagic fever as a public health problem in the Americas. *Infectious Agents and Disease* **26**:383-93.

Guerrant, Richard L. 1997. Cryptospoidiosis: An emerging, highly infectious threat. *Emerg. Inf. Dis.* **3:** No 1.

Hedburg,, C.W., W.C. Levine, K.E. White, R.H. Carleson, D.K. Winsor, D.N. Cameron, K.L. MacDonald, and M.T. Osterholm. 1992. An international food borne outbreak of Shigellosis associated with a commercial airline. *JAMA* **268**:: 3208-3212.

Hiramatsu, Keiichi. 1997. Vancomycin resistant *Staphylococcus aureus*. *J. Antimicrobial Chemotherapy*. (In press).

Hughes, J., 1995. Emerging infectious diseases: Meeting the challenge. 1995 Conference on Emerging Infectious Disease.

Huq, A., R.R. Colwell, M.A.R. Chowdhury, B. Xu, S.M. Moniruezaman, M.S. Islam, M. Yunus, and M.S. Albert. 1995. Coexistence of *Vibrio cholerae* 01 and 0139 Bengal in Bangladesh. *Lancet* **345**: 1249.

Kramer, M.H., Herwaldt, B.L., Craun, G.F., Calderon, R.L., Juranek, D.D. 1996. Surveillance for water borne-disease outbreaks --- United States, 1993-1994. *MMWR Morb Mortal Wkly Rep* **45**: 1-22.

Krause, R.M. 1992. The origin of plagues: old and new. *Science* **257**:1073-8.

Kuo, C., Shor, A., Campbell, L.A. *et al*, 1993. Demonstration of Chlamydia pneumoniae in atherosclerotic lesions of coronary arteries, *J Infect Dis* **167**:841-9.

LeChevallier, M.W., Schulz, W., Lee, R.G. 1991. Bacterial nutrients in drinking water. *Appl. Environ. Microbiol.* **57**: 857-862.

Lederberg,, J. 1988. Medical science, infectious disease, and the unity of humankind. *JAMA* **260**:684-5.

Levy, S.B., 1993. Confronting multidrug resistance: a role for each of us. *JAMA* **269**:1840-2.

MacKenzie, W.R., Hoxie, N.J., Proctor, M.E. *et al.* 1994. A Massive outbreak in Milwaukee of Cryptosporidium infection transmitted through the public water supply. *N. Engl. J. Med.* **331**:161-7.

MacKenzie, W.R., Hoxie, N.J., Proctor, M.E., Gradus, M.S., Blair, K.A., Peterson, D.E., *et al.* 1994. A massive outbreak in Milwaukee of *Cryptosporidium* infection transmitted through the public water supply. *N. Engl. J. Med.* **331**: 161-167.

Marsh, K., M. English, J. Crawley, and N. Peshu. 1996. The pathogenesis of severe malaria in African children. *Ann. Trop. Med. Parasitol.* **90**: 395-4002.

Meslin, F.-X. 1997. Global aspects of emerging and potential zoonoses: a WHO perspective. *Emerg. Inf. Dis.* **3:** No 2.

Michele, T.M.,W.A. Cronin, N.M.H. Graham, *et al* 1997. Transmission of *Mycobacterium tuberculosis* by a fiberoptic bronchoscope: DNA fingerprinting. *JAMA* **278**:1093-1095.

Millard, P.S., Gensheimer, K.F., Addiss, D.G., Sosin, D.M., Beckett, G.A., Houck-Jankoski, A., *et al.* 1994. An outbreak of cryptosporidiosis from fresh-pressed apple cider. *JAMA* **272(20)**: 1592-1596.

Morse, S.S. 1991. Emerging viruses: defining the rules for viral traffic. *Perspect Biol Med* **34**:387 409.

Morse, S.S., Schluederberg, A. 1990. Emerging viruses: the evolution of viruses and viral diseases. *J. Infect. Dis.* **162**:1-7.

Morse, S.S. 1991. Emerging viruses: Defining the rules for viral traffic. *Perspect Biol Med* **34**:387 409.

Morse, S.S. 1993. Examining the origins of emerging viruses. In: Morse SS, ed. Emerging viruses. New York: Oxford University Press, 10-28.

Morse, S.S. 1995. Factors in the emergence of infectious diseases. *Emerg. Inf. Dis.* **1**: 7-15.

Neill, M.A., Rice, S.K., Ahmad, N.V., Flanigan, T.P. 1996. Cryptosporidiosisan unrecognized cause of diarrhea in elderly hospitalized patients. *Clin. Infect. Dis.* **22**: 168-170.

Neu, H.C. 1992. The crisis in the antibiotic resistance. *Science* **257**:1064-72.

Palmer, R., E. Drinan, and T. Murphy. 1994. A previously unknown disease of farmed Atlantic salmon: pathology and establishment of bacterial etiology. *Dis. Aquat. Org.* **19**: 7-14.

Patuwatama, S., W.H. Thompson, D.M. Watts, and R.P. Hanson. 1992. Experimental infection of chipmunks and squirrels with LaCrosse and trevettatus viruses. *Am. J. Trop. Med. Hyg.* **21**: 476-481.

Regnery, R. and J. Tapparo. 1995. Unraveling mysteries associated with cat-scratch disease, bacillary angiomatosis, and related syndromes. *J. Inf. Dis.* **1**: 16-21.

Riley, L.W., R.S. Remis, S.D. Helgerson, *et al.* 1983. Hemorrhagic colitis associated with a rare *Escerchia coli* serotype. *N. Eng. J. Med.* **308**: 681-685.

Rogers, D.J., Packer, M.J. 1993. Vector-borne diseases, models, and global change. *Lancet* **342**:1282-4.

Rothenberger, N. 1994. Cryptosporidium: Information on water borne outbreak in Milwaukee. *CDC-MMWR* **42**: 53-57.

Rwaguma, E.B., J. J. Lutwama, S.D.K. Sempala, *et al.* 1997. Emergence of O''nyong-nyong fever in southwestern Uganda after an abscence of 35 years. *Emerg. Inf. Dis.* **3**: No 1.

Satcher, D. 1995. Emerging infections: Getting ahead of the curve. *Emerg. Inf. Dis.* **1**: 1-6.

Scholtissek, C., Naylor, E. 1988. Fish farming and influenza pandemics. *Nature* **331**:215.

Shope, R.E. 1997. Arborviruses as sentinel infections for ecological change. Emerging Infections Information Network Spring 1997 Seminar. **http:://info.med.yale.edu/EIINet**

Simon, Jeffrey D. 1997. Biological terrorism - preparing to meet the threat. *JAMA* **278**: 428-430.

Snow, J. 1854. *On the Epidemic of Cholera.* Commonwealth Publishers, New York. (Reprinted, 1936).

Steidenger, K.A., H.B. Burkholer, *et al* 1996. *Pfiesteria piscicida*, a new toxic dinoflagellate genus and species in the order Dinamoebales. *J. Phycol.* **32**:157-164.

Swerdlow, David L., E.D. Mintz, M. Rodriguez, *et al.* 1992. Waterborne transmission of epidemic cholera in Trujillo, Peru: lessons for a continent at risk. *The Lancet.* **340**: 28-32.

Tauxe, R.V., E.D. Mintz, and R.E. Quick. 1995. Epidemic cholera in the New World: translating epidemiology into new prevention strategies. *Emerg. Inf. Dis.* **1**: No 1.

Texas Natural Resource Conservation Commission, 1995. State of Texas Water Quality Inventory, 12th Edition, 175-177-TNRCC, Austin Tx.

Wenzel, R.P. and M.B. Edmond. 1997. Tuberculosis infection after bronchoscopy. *JAMA* **278**:1111.

Wilson, M. E., R. Levins, and A. Spielman, 1994. Detection, surveillance, and response to emerging diseases. *N.Y. Acad. Sci.* **70**: 336-338.

World Health Organization. 1996. Ebola haemorrhagic fever - South Africa. *Wkly. Epidemiol. Rec.* **71**: 359.

World Health Organization. 1996. Ebola haemorrhagic fever -- Gabon. *Wkly. Epidemiol. Rec.* **71**: 320.

World Health Organization. 1996. Outbreak of Ebola haemorrhagic fever in Gabon officially declared over. *Wkly. Epidemiol. Rec.* **71**: 125-126.

World Health Organization. 1997. Ebola haemorrhagic fever. *Wkly. Epidemiol. Rec.* **72**: 7.

Yamanaishi, K., Okuno, T., Shiraki, K., Takahashi, M., Kondo, T., Asano, Y., Kurata, T. 1988. Identification of human herpesvirus-6 as a causal agent for exanthem subitum. *Lancet* **1**:1065-7.

Yamanishi, K., Okuno, T., Shiraki, K. *et al*. 1988. Identification of human herpesvirus-6 as a casual agent for exanthem subitum. *Lancet* **1**:1065-7.

Yang, X.B. and H. Scherm. 1997. El Niño and infectious disease. *Science* **275**: 5301.

Appendix A

Glossary

Acute infection - a disease with a short severe course.

Adulterant - Any substance added to food which makes the food unfit for consumption.

Carrier - a person who harbors a pathogen without showing symptoms of it, but is capable of transmitting it to another.

Chronic infection - a prolonged long-lasting disease.

Clade - a group of viruses which share a common ancestor.

Enteric - pertaining to the lower digestive tract.

Epidemic - An unusually high incidence of a disease.

Epidemiology - All the factors related to the spread of a disease.

Epizootic - An epidemic in a lower animal population.

Etiology - the cause of a disease.

Febrile - With fever.

Fomite - Any inanimate object which harbors pathogens.

Fulminating - Occurring with unusual rapidity.

Gastroenteritis - Inflammation of the digestive tract.

Index outbreak - An unusual incidence which calls attention to a disease.

Morbidity - The incidence of a disease in a population, usually expressed as the number of cases per 10,000.

Mortality- the death rate of a disease in a population, usually expressed as the number of deaths per 10,000 cases.

Nosocomial - Refers to infections acquired in a hospital or other health care facility.

Pandemic - A world-wide epidemic.

Parasite - An organism that lives in or on a host.

Pathogen - An organism which causes a disease.

Point source outbreak - high morbidity originating from a single definable source or event.

Prodromal period - the time following invasion by a pathogen before a host shows symptoms.

Prions - infectious protein particles.

Prognosis - the usual expected outcome of a disease.

Serologic - Technically, the study of blood serum; now applied to procedures for identification of microbial proteins.

Subclinical - A disease which does not produce symptoms.

Transposons - Engineered mobile portions of genes.

Vector - An organism, usually insect, which transmits a pathogen that is not itself affected.

Venereal Transmission - Acquisition of a disease through sexual relations.

Viroid - An infectious short RNA not covered with a protein coat.

Virulence - The intensity of the infective process.

Xenograft - Transplantation of tissue from another species.

Xenozoonosis - Disease communicated to recipient species by xenograft.

Zoonosis - Disease naturally communicable from lower animals to man.

Appendix B

Abbreviations

AMA - American Medical Association

APHA - American Public Health Association

ASM - American Society for Microbiology

BSE - Bovine Spongiform Encephalopathy

CDC - Communicable Disease Center - now Center for Disease Control

CVV - Cache Valley Virus

EID - Emerging Infectious Diseases

ENT - ear, nose, and throat

FDA - Food and drug administration

GI - gastrointestinal

IgG - Immune globulin G

LD - Lethal dosage

MMWR - Morbidity/Mortality Weekly Report

MPN - most probable number

NIAID - Natural Institute for Allergy and Infectious Disease

OEI - Office Epizootics Interrnationale

PAHO - Pan American Health Organization

PCR - Polymerization chain reaction

PID - Pelvic Inflammatory Disease

STD - Sexually Transmitted Disease

UG - urogenital

UK - United Kingdom

UR - upper respiratory

USPHS - United States Public Health Service

VEE - Venezuelan equine encephalitis

WHO - World Health Organization (of the United Nations)

Appendix C

Internet Resources for New and Emerging Diseases

A characteristic of the internet is constant change. Some of the URL's listed here may be obsolete by the time this book is printed. We have tried to select sites such as government and other agencies that are likely to be around for some time and have links to other pages. Hopefully, this list will be a good starting point for those seeking current information.

All the virology on the www
http://www.tulane.edu/~dmsander/garryfavweb.html

Balogh Scientific Books
ftp://ftp.balogh.com/pub/users/balogh/catalogs/indiamed.html

BIOSCI/bionet Electronic Newsgroup Network for Biology
http://www.bio.net

Emerging and Re-emerging viruses: AN ESSAY
http://www.bocklabs.wisc.edu/ed/ebola.html

Emerging Infections Information Network
http://info.med.yale.edu/EIINET/welcome.html

Emerging Infectious Diseases
http://www.cdc.gov/ncidod/EID/eid.htm

Emerging Infectious Diseases
http://www.cdc.gov/ncidod/EID

European Network for Antibiotic Resistance and Epidemiology
http://info.rivm.nl/enare

FAS Program for Monitoring Emerging Diseases (ProMED)
http://www.fas.org/promed/

Infectious Diseases Society of America
http://www.idsociety.org.:80/RETRO.HTM

Institute of molecular Virology
http://sss.bocklabs.wisc.edu/welcome.html

LB13. Human Infection with SIV: Role of net and its
Implications for Live Viral Attenuation
http://www.idsociety.org.:80/abst/599.htm

Morbidity and Mortality Weekly Report
http://www.cdc.gov/epo/mmwr/mmwr.html

Medical Microbiology Websites
http://biomed.nus.sg/microbio/home.html

MedWeb: Tropical Medicine
http://www.cc.emory.edu/WHSCL/medweb.tropmed.html

National Institute of Allergy and Infectious Diseases
http://www.niaid.nih.gov

National Institute of Animal Health (Japan)
http://ss.niah.affrc.go.jp/

Office International des Epizooties (OIE)
http://www.oie.org/

Outbreak - Active outbreaks
http://www.outbreak.org/   dynaserve.exe/outbreaks.html#ecoli-scot

PAHO - Home Page
http://www.paho.org/

PAHO - Quick Reference List
http://www.paho.org/english/db16c-po.htm#QuickReference

PAHO - Regional Plan for Emerging and Re-Emerging Diseases
http://www.paho.org/english/hcteme02.htm

Pan American Health Organization
http://www.paho.org/english/DPI

Parasitology Information
http://jeffline.tju.edu/CWIS/OAC/microweb/parasitology/

Pathogenesis I
http://glindquester.biology.rhodes.edu/seniorseminar/cellpath-h/cellpath.html

Pfiesteria website
http://www.mdsg.umd.edu/fish-health/pfiesteria/

ProMED
http://www.fas.org/promed/

ProMED
http://www.healthnet.org/promed.html

ProMED - mail: Plant Diseases Announcements (Chronological)
http://www.agnic.org/pmp/index.html

SurfSites for CyberBiologists
http://ucsu.colorado.edu/~marcora/surf.htm

The Alternative Medicine Homepage
http://www.pitt.edu/~cbw/altm.html

The American Society for Microbiology
http://www.asmusa.org

The DNA Vaccine Web
http://www.genweb.com/Dnavax/main.html

The National Prevention Agency Centers for Disease Control
and Prevention
http://www.cdc.gov/

The Tick Research Laboritory
http://www.uri.edu/artsci/zool/ticklab

The World Wide Virtual Library
http://golgi.harvard.edu/biopages/biochem.html

TMRMC Health and Medical Links
http://www.tmrmc.com/textonly/links.htm#disease

UNTHSC International Travel Medicine Clinic (ITMC)
http://www.hsc.unt.edu/clinics/itmc/travel.htm

Vector-borne Diseases and Climate Change
http://www.ciesin.org/TG/HH/veclev2.html

Virology Websites
http://www.tulane.edu/%7Edmsander/garryfavwebindexhtml

Viruses: Risks and Benefits of Society
**http://glindquester.biology.rhodes.edu/seniorseminar/seniors-
eminar.html**

Welcome to CDC WONDER on the Web
http://wonder.cdc.gov/

WHO: Emerging and Other Communicable Diseases
http://www.who.ch/programmes/emc/news.html

World Health Organization www Home Page
http://www.who.ch/

INDEX

A

Acute infection 47, 64, 117
Acyclovir 61
Adulterant 117
Aedes aegypti 94
Aedes taeniorhynchus 90
Africa 72, 79, 80, 94, 102, 107, 116
American Medical Association 89, 120
American Public Health Association 120
American Social Health Association 61
American Society for Microbiology 120, 124
Andes Virus 65, 67
Anopheles 71, 72, 103
Argentina 47, 65
Arizona 47
Asymptomatic shedding 61
Australia 28, 55, 102
Avian Influenza H5N1 .... 3, 31

B

Bartonella henselae 110
Bird flu 31
Bovine Spongiform Encephalopathy 33, 120
Brazil 25, 51
Bunyaviruses 37, 38, 40

C

Cache Valley Virus 37, 38, 111, 120
California 47, 48
Carrier 85, 117
Center for Disease Control 79, 120
Central America 43, 47, 94
Chlamydia 41, 42, 103, 112

Chlamydial Infections..41, 42
Cholera.....................................28, 43, 44, 45, 92, 110, 107, 115
Chronic infection 117
Clade 67, 117
Coccidioides immitis 47
Coccidioidomycosis..47, 48, 49
Colorado State University...104
Columbia...26, 90
Consumption 86
Coxsackie virus..74, 75
Cryptosporidiosis...50, 52, 110, 113
Cryptosporidium parvum 50
Cuba...94
Cyclosporal diarrhea 16
Cyst..63

D
Dengue 55, 56, 74,104, 107, 111

E
El Niño...28, 116
England 33, 35, 85, 104
Enteric...84, 117
Epidemic 23, 24, 27, 28, 31, 40, 43, 44, 53, 65,
70, 79, 95, 102, 111, 115, 117, 118
Epidemiology.......35, 44, 53, 61, 67, 73, 105, 110, 115, 117, 122
Epizootic 90, 117
Equador 90
Escherichia coli...16, 57
Etiology.....................................24, 40, 74, 79, 114, 117
Europe..47, 86
European Molecular Biology laboratory 103

F

Febrile 117
Federal Emergency Management Administration 100
Fomite 52, 117
Fulminating 117

G

Galloping consumption 86
Genital 60, 61, 62, 78, 103
Germany 43
Giardia lamblia 63
Giardiasis 63, 64
Gonorrhea 42
Greece 55

H

Hantavirus 65
Hawaiian Islands 47
Heidelberg 103
Hemolytic uremic syndrome 57, 109
Hepatitis 16, 23, 73
Herpes Simplex Virus 60
herpesvirus 116
Hong Kong 12, 31, 74
Human immunodeficiency virus 56

I

Immune globulin G 120
Index outbreak 26, 117
Influenza 9, 10, 11, 31, 90, 115
Italy 47

J

Japan 55, 123

K
Korea 67

L
Legionella pneumophila 68
Legionnaires' Disease 68
Liverpool School of Tropical Medicine 104
London 43, 55
Lymphogranuloma venereum 41

M
Mad Cow Disease 16, 22, 33
Maine 52
Malaria 23, 28, 29, 70, 71, 72, 73, 103, 104, 107, 113
Malaysia 74
Mali 73
Mexico 55
Morbidity 20, 79, 103, 118, 120, 123
Mycobacterium tuberculosis 86, 109, 113
Myocarditis 74

N
New Guinea 34
North America 38, 90, 94, 102
Nosocomial 68, 69, 76, 77, 89, 98, 118

P
Pan American Health Organization 120, 124
Panama 90, 94
Pandemic 9, 12, 31, 118
Parasite 63, 73, 104, 118
Pathogen 19, 38, 117, 118
Peru 43, 44, 115
Pfiesteria piscicida 81, 115
Pfiesteriosis 3, 81
Plasmodium falciparum 70
Plasmodium malariae 70

Plasmodium ovale 70
Point source outbreak... 52, 118
Prodromal period 118
Prognosis... 106, 118
Prostatitis 82, 83

Q
Queen Mary Hospital.. 74

S
Salmonella.. 13, 84
Sarawak..74, 75
Sexually Transmitted Disease... 41, 121
Shigilla sonnei... 26
Sibu 74
Sin Nombre virus 67
South America 28, 48, 56, 90, 94
Staphylococcus aureus 77, 112
Staphylococcus epidermidis... 78
Subclinical.. 42, 47, 95, 118

T
Texas.......................... 19, 21, 23, 25, 37, 38, 40, 47, 55, 111, 115
The Royal College of Physicians... 55
Toxoplasmosis 23
Transmissible Spongiform
Encephalopathy.. 33
Transposons 104, 118
Trinidad.. 90
Trophozoite 63
Tuberculosis.. 86, 88, 89, 101, 115

U
United Kingdom.. 33, 121
United States 25, 34, 38, 41, 47, 51, 55, 56, 57,
60, 64, 66, 67, 70, 72, 74, 86, 90, 100, 110, 112, 121

V
Vancomycin 76, 77, 112
Vector.......................... 28, 56, 90, 91, 94, 95, 104, 118
Venereal Transmission... 118
Venezuelan Equine Encephalitis...................... 90, 121
Vibrio cholerae.. 43, 109, 112
Vibrio vulnificus 92
Virulence.. 91, 96, 119

W
World Health Organization.............. 2, 3, 22, 33, 74, 95, 102, 116, 121, 125

X
Xenograft 119
Xenozoonosis.. 21, 22, 119

Y
Yellow Fever... 74, 94, 95, 107
Yucatan 94

Z
Zoonosis... 21, 22, 119